Chindian Myth of Mulian Rescuing His Mother – On Indic Origins of the *Yulanpen Sūtra*

Chindian Myth of Mulian Rescuing His Mother – On Indic Origins of the *Yulanpen Sūtra*

Debate and Discussion

Xiaohuan Zhao

ANTHEM PRESS

Anthem Press
An imprint of Wimbledon Publishing Company
www.anthempress.com

This edition first published in UK and USA 2023
by ANTHEM PRESS
75–76 Blackfriars Road, London SE1 8HA, UK
or PO Box 9779, London SW19 7ZG, UK
and
244 Madison Ave #116, New York, NY 10016, USA

British Library Cataloguing-in-Publication Data
A catalogue record for this book is available from the British Library.

Library of Congress Cataloging-in-Publication Data
A catalog record for this book has been requested.
2023937007

ISBN-13: 978-1-83998-696-3 (pbk)
ISBN-10: 1-83998-696-4 (pbk)

Cover image: *Mulian Saves His Mother.* Scroll painting. Anonymous (fl. 19th century).
Source: http://academic.reed.edu/hellscrolls/scrolls/Aseries/A10/A10c.html

This title is also available as an e-book.

Once Again
To
My Wife
This Book
Is
Affectionately Dedicated

CONTENTS

LIST OF FIGURES

PREFACE

This book is an outgrowth of a research project I began in 2016 on Nuo theatre (Nuoxi) and Mulian theatre (Mulianxi), the two most representative forms of Chinese temple theatre. Mulianxi is the oldest living Buddhist ritual drama with more than nine hundred years of performance history. At the heart of Mulianxi is the myth of Mulian recusing his mother from Hell, which finds expression in almost all forms of traditional Chinese performance literature and performing arts including Xiqu or Chinese opera. As such, Mulianxi stands as a living testimony of the historical development of Xiqu from myth to ritual and from ritual drama to drama.

My search for the origins of the Mulian myth led me first to the *Yulanpen jing* or *Yulanpen Sūtra*, the earliest known Buddhist scripture that features Mulian as a filial son, a devout monk and an epic hero adventuring into Hell to save his mother. At the outset, I took the view widely held among scholars and students of Chinese Buddhism that the scripture was a Chinese Buddhist composition, but when I dug into Chinese Buddhist catalogues for its record alongside relevant Indic sources, Buddhist and non-Buddhist, I became suspicious. Indeed, the deeper I dug, the deeper suspicion I had of the widely held view. Thus, began my years of journey of exploring the Indic origins of the sūtra and the myth. The journey has now come to an end with this book.

Consisting of four chapters in addition to Introduction and Conclusion, the book starts with a quick survey of the history of Yulanpen/Zhongyuan/Ghost Festival in China, followed by a brief introduction to its scriptural source, that is, the *Yulanpen Sūtra*, scholarly opinions on the authenticity/inauthenticity of the sūtra, the central argument of the book and the strategy for developing the argument in the book. The last section of Introduction is a discussion and explanation of key terms such as 'apocryphal scripture', 'doubtful scripture', '(literal, free, creative, text-oriented and reader-oriented) translation', 'localisation' and 'sinicisation', which constitute the basis for the development of the argument.

Chapter 1 begins with an annotated English translation of the sūtra from Chinese, followed by a brief survey of Mulian (Skr. Maudgalyāyana; Pāli:

Moggallāna) as a historical figure in Indian Buddhist literature, particularly in its Theravāda tradition. Chapters 2 and 3 are devoted respectively to an etymological exploration of the keywords in the sūtra, that is, *yulan*, *pen* and *yulanpen* and a thorough examination of the sūtra in Buddhist catalogues and bibliographies from medieval China. The backbone of this book is Chapter 4, which begins with a critical review of major arguments against the authenticity of the sūtra and proceeds to a point-by-point refutation and rebuttal of them based on both internal and external evidence. The book then comes to a conclusion with a summary of the major arguments for the Indic origins of the sūtra and myth.

In the course of exploring the Indic origins of the *Yulanpen Sūtra* and the Mulian myth, I received help from numerous people. I would particularly like to say thank you to Jinhua Jia, Mark Allon and Seishi Karashima (1957–2019) for reading early drafts of the book manuscript and offering comments and suggestions, to Huang Yongfeng, Jason Tai and Phra Kiattisak Kittipanyo for providing me with photographs pertaining to this study, and to the University of Sydney China Studies Centre (CSC) and FASS School of Languages and Cultures (SLC) for providing support at different stages of this research project. I would also like to take this opportunity to express my gratitude to the anonymous peer reviewers of the book proposal and book manuscript for their extremely encouraging and insightful feedback and to the Anthem Acquisition and Editorial Support, particularly Jebaslin Hephzibah, Megan Greiving, Mario Rosair and Jessica Mack for their timely response to my enquiries concerning manuscription preparation and submission. Chapter 1 is adapted from Zhao (2021a). To Routledge, Taylor & Francis Group, I express my appreciation for granting me the permission to adapt and republish it in this book. It is my pleasure to acknowledge all the help I have received in getting the manuscript ready to submit, and I alone am responsible for whatever errors remain.

AUTHOR'S NOTES

For premodern Chinese texts, they are cited by title rather than by author. In such cases, the scroll (*juan*) number is also given, followed by period and page number. Some texts reprinted in traditional folio format, in pages with flattened recto/verso sides (often with more than one to a page), are also given sequential pagination in Arabic numerals. In such cases, the scroll and page number (with recto/verso indication) of the traditional format is cited.

Unless otherwise noted, the Chinese Buddhist texts including those in the Taishō Tripiṭaka I quote and refer to throughout this book are all taken from and numbered according to the Chinese Electronic Tripiṭaka Collection (http://www.cbeta.org/) developed by Chinese Buddhist Electronic Text Association (CBETA). Take for example the entry for Faxian (337–422) in the *Biographies of Eminent Monks* (*Gaoseng zhuan*, T50n2059_003.0337b19). In the parenthesis, the number after *T* is the sequential number of the cited text in the Taishō Tripiṭaka (*Taishō shinshu daizōkyō*), which consists of the volume number (the number before *n*) and the text number (the number after *n*); the number following the underscore is the scroll number of the cited text; the number after the full stop is the page number in that volume; the letter after the page number is the horizontal register (*a*, *b* or *c*) on that page; and the number after the register indication is the column number in that register.

The Daoist scriptures I quote and refer to throughout this book are all taken from the Baiyunguan version of the *Zhengtong Daozang* or *Daoist Canon Compiled During the Zhengtong Reign Period* [1436–1449].

The definition and translation of Buddhist terms are based on Buswell and Lopez (2013) unless otherwise stated. A Sanskrit style of orthography as in Monier-Williams (2003) is observed throughout in spelling Indic words and expressions unless they come from direct quotations or originate from Pāli texts.

For Chinese romanisation, Pinyin (without tone mark) is used throughout the book except in direct quotations. No Chinese characters are provided in the main text or endnotes for Chinese terms unless necessary to avoid confusion. Instead, a glossary for them is provided at the end of the book, where Pinyin is given followed by the *fantizi* (traditional scripts) even if originally published in *jiantizi* (simplified scripts). Likewise, only Romaji or Romaja is given in the running text and endnotes for Japanese and Korean terms with their form in Kanji/Kana or Hanja/Hangul provided in the glossary as are their Chinese counterparts.

Non-English words and expressions are italicised throughout the book except for proper nouns; Latin terms that are common in the English language; and words used many times after the first usage.

INTRODUCTION

The earliest known official Yulanpen Ceremony was held at the Monastery of Universal Tranquility (Tongtai si, see Figure 0.1) in Jiankang, the capital city of the Liang dynasty (502–557), in 538 or the fourth year of Datong during the reign of Emperor Wu of Liang (Liang Wudi, r. 502–549) (*Fozu tongji*, T49n2035_037.351a26). The ceremony soon spread across the country, developed into a grand religious festival – the Yulanpen Festival (*Yulanpen jie*) – of making offerings to buddhas and bodhisattvas, Daoist gods and priests, deified ancestors, and orphaned souls and wild ghosts (*guhun yegui*) on the fifteenth day of the seventh lunisolar month, and has since been observed nationwide in China and beyond. At the core of the festival is the myth of Mulian (Skr. Maudgalyāyana; Pāli: Moggallāna) adventuring into the realm of hungry ghosts (Skr. *preta*; Ch. *egui*) to rescue his mother.

The primary source for the Mulian myth is the *Yulanpen Sūtra Expounded by the Buddha* (*Fo shuo Yulanpen jing*, T16n0685), which is traditionally attributed to

Figure 0.1 First constructed in 300 during the Western Jin dynasty (265–316), the Cockcrow Monastery (Jimingsi si) was converted into an office for the Commandant of the Court (*tingwei*) during the Eastern Jin dynasty (317–420). In the first year (527) of Datong, Emperor Wu chose the site for constructing the Tongtai si, which was reconstructed and renamed Jiming si as per imperial decree in the twentieth year (1387) of Hongwu in the Ming dynasty (1368–1644). Photo by the author.

the Indo-Scythian Dharmarakṣa (aka Zhu Tanmoluocha, better known as Zhu Fahu, d. 308) as its translator. Beginning in the sixth century, various references to the sūtra and the ceremony/festival appeared in both Buddhist and non-Buddhist literature. In an early sixth-century Buddhist encyclopaedia titled *Differentiated Manifestations of the Sūtra and Vinaya Piṭaka* (*Jinglü yixiang*, T53n2121_014.0073c22), for example, the sūtra was given as the scriptural source for the ceremony of making Yulanpen offerings on the fifteenth day of the seventh month.

The ceremony was also mentioned by Yan Zhitui (531–591), a prominent scholar-official who served four different, short-lived dynasties during the Northern and Southern Dynasties (420–589). In the 'Chapter on the Final Disposition' ('Zhongzhi pian'), the twentieth and final chapter of his *Family Instructions for the Yan Clan* (*Yanshi jiaxun* 7.602), Yan writes:

> Sacrifices should be performed in four seasons as per the teachings of Duke Zhou and Confucius in order for descendants not to forget their deceased parents and their filial obligation. According to the [Buddhist] Inner Canon (*neidian*), however, it does one no good [to sacrifice], for killing living things would instead add to one's sins. To repay the boundless kindness of one's parents and express sorrow and grief for them, one should make vegetarian offerings from time to time and also make the Mid-Seventh Month Yulanpen offerings. This is what you are expected of.

This is the earliest recorded reference to the Yulanpen Ceremony/Festival as 'Mid-Seventh Month' (*Qiyue ban*), which later became a popular name of the Yulanpen/Zhongyuan/Ghost Festival in China.

In the *Record of the Festivals and Seasonal Customs of the Jing-Chu Region* (*Jing-Chu suishi ji* 1.22b), Zong Lin (498–561) created an entry for the Yulanpen Festival, which reads: 'Buddhist monks and nuns, Daoist priests and laypeople all make Yulanpen offerings to buddhas on the fifteenth day of the seventh month'. Significantly, the entry comes complete in its received text with an annotation provided by Du Gongzhan, a Sui dynasty (581–618) scholar-official, who quoted a portion of the *Yulanpen Sūtra* in his commentary on the *Jing-Chu suishi ji* (1.23a).

All this suggests that the Mulian myth alongside the sūtra had been widely circulated on both sides of the Yangtze River by the end of the sixth century, when the Buddhist Yulanpen Ceremony had become a nationwide religious festival observed by all, including both the (Buddhist and Daoist) clergy and the laity.

For nearly six centuries from the late Western Jin (AD 265–316) through the Tang dynasty (618–907), more than twenty works were produced that dealt with the Mulian myth, and the Song (960–1279) and later dynasties witnessed the appearance of dozens of more such works (Mair 1986–1987: 84). They came in large numbers and appeared in various art forms and renditions, accounting for the enormous popularity of the Mulian myth and Yulanpen Festival at different levels of society in medieval China (Teiser 1988).

It is commonly accepted that the scriptural source of the Yulanpen Festival is the *Yulanpen Sūtra* (see Figure 0.2), which, however, is overwhelmingly regarded as a Chinese Buddhist apocryphal scripture in modern Chinese, Japanese and Western scholarship for its thematic emphasis on 'Confucian' filial piety and ancestor worship, among others. Nonetheless, there is no shortage of research on the authenticity of the *Yulanpen Sūtra* as an Indian Buddhist scripture, as shown in Chen (1999), Wu (2001), Fujimoto (2003), Xing (2011) and Karashima (2013b). These studies all offer invaluable insights here and there into the translation and transmission of the sūtra, but they tend to aim at limited aspects of the scriptural text, leaving others untouched. As a result, we are still not clear or certain about the authenticity of the *Yulanpen Sūtra*, let alone the Indic origins of the sūtra and Mulian myth. The fierce controversy surrounding this Buddhist scripture remains and rages on, highlighting the urgent need for a systematic study of the scripture.

This study aims to clarify points of suspicion and controversy and benefit research of this nature in the future. While building on the existing debate and discussion, this book is devoted to a thorough examination of the text and context of the *Yulanpen Sūtra* in the light of all the major arguments against its authenticity. I argue that the storyline and subject matter of the Mulian myth are well rooted in Indian culture and literature and that it is more

Figure 0.2 Rubbing of Tang dynasty (618–907) stone inscription of the *Yulanpen Sūtra* from Shrine 141 of Gongxian Caves, Henan Province. Size: 47.5 cm × 107.5 cm. Photo by the author.

likely that the *Yulanpen Sūtra* is a Chinese creative translation rather than an indigenous Chinese composition.

This is a multi-disciplinary project that involves history, religion, etymology, translation, bibliology and bibliography, exegesis and textual criticism and cross-cultural and comparative studies. For the presentation and development of the argument, the classical model for argumentation will be adopted, hence a sequence-structure arranged roughly in the order of Introduction (*Exordium*); Statement of Background (*Narratio*); Proposition (*Propositio*); Proof (*Confirmatio*); Refutation (*Refuatio*) and Conclusion (*Peroratio*). The rest of the book is thus organised as follows. First, I provide an English translation of the *Yulanpen Sūtra* before I examine Mulian or Maudgalyāyana portrayed in Indian Buddhist literature as a chief disciple of the Buddha. Next, I review etymological studies of the words, *yulan*, *pen* and *yulanpen.* I then carry out a full investigation into the *Yulanpen Sūtra* recorded in Buddhist catalogues from medieval China. After presenting major arguments prevalent in modern scholarship against the authenticity of the sūtra, I refute and rebut them point by point based on both internal and external evidence. Finally, I draw a conclusion on the Indic origins of the *Yulanpen Sùtra* and the Mulian myth.

To begin at the beginning, I would like to define several key terms in the argument so as to have a meaningful debate and discussion. Let me start with the word, 'apocrypha'. Derived from Greek *apokryptein*, meaning 'to hide away', this biblical term is borrowed into Chinese Buddhist studies to designate Buddhist works which claim to be authentic or true scriptures translated directly from Indic sources, although they were actually composed in China on the model of Indian Buddhist scriptures (Buswell 1990: 3–7; Muller 1998: 63–66; Hureau 2009), or put it in the words of Lopez (2016: 6), 'works composed beyond the borders of India that purport to be Indian works'. Apocryphal scriptures are collectively referred to in the Chinese Buddhist bibliography as *yiwei jing* with *yijing* denoting 'doubtful scriptures' or 'scriptures of dubious origin' and *weijing* 'forged or fabricated scriptures'.

Makita Tairyō (1985: 286) classifies Buddhist scriptures of dubious origin into three types, i.e. scriptures that are concerned with Daoist talismans and auguries, and esoteric techniques; scriptures that are concerned with the strange and supernatural in Chinese folk beliefs and practices; and scriptures that contain respectable contents compatible with Buddhism and/or Chinese indigenous thoughts and teachings such as the *Scripture on the Profundity of Parental Kindness* (*Fumu enzhong jing*).

Wang Wenyan (1997: 25–40) identifies three major sources for Chinese Buddhist apocrypha, namely, (1) regression and revelation (*suxi mingshou*); (2) quotation and redaction (*chaolu*); and (3) forgery and fabrication (*weizao*). Apocryphal scriptures created by means of 'regression and revelation' are those recited from memory and written down as scriptures by Buddhist followers who claim to have learnt the scripture in a previous life of theirs or those revealed by a Buddha or Bodhisattva to them through dreams and visions. Most famous of this type apocryphal scriptures are the twenty-one scriptures in thirty-five scrolls (*juan*) recited by Sengfa, the young daughter of Jiang Mi who was an Erudite Fellow of the Imperial Academy (*taixue boshi*) in the Southern Qi dynasty (479–502) (*Chu Sanzang jiji*, T55n2145_005.0040a07–0040b06), and the *Avalokiteśvara Sūtra of King Gao* (*Gaowang Guanshiyin jing*), which was attributed to a Northern Qi dynasty (550–577) prisoner on death row, who is said to have dreamed – on the night before the execution – of a spirit-monk (*shenseng*) revealing to him the scripture and requesting him to recite by heart for several thousand times so as to be released and pardoned from capital punishment (*Da Zhou kanding zhongjing mulu*, T55n2153_007.0416a02).[1] The second major source of apocryphal scriptures are texts quoted and redacted from genuine scriptures before being collected and edited into a 'scripture' (*jing*) under a title different from that of their original source(s), such as the thirty-six scriptures hand-copied by Xiao Ziliang (460–494), King Wenxuan of Jingling (*Chu Sanzang jiji*, T55n2145_005.0037c01). Scriptures, such as the *Sūtra Expounded by the Buddha in Forty-Two Sections* (*Fo shuo sishi'er zhang jing*), the *Scripture of Laozi Converting the Barbarians* (*Laozi huahu jing*) and the *Scripture on the Original Vows of the Bodhisattva Kṣitigarbha* (*Dizang pusa benyuan jing*), were forged or fabricated by a Buddhist follower or a Buddhist sect to promote their own belief and teaching, and they account for the bulk of the apocryphal scriptures listed in Chinese Buddhist bibliography. Identified as apocryphal in the *Comprehensive Catalogue of the Scriptures* (*Zongli zhongjing mulu*), the earliest known catalogue of Chinese Buddhist texts compiled by the Eastern Jin monk Dao'an (314–385), are twenty-six titles in thirty scrolls (*Chu sanzang jiji*, T55n2145_005.0038b08–0038c16), and the number of apocryphal scriptures dramatically increases to 407 titles in a total of 1,510 scrolls as listed in the *Catalogue of the Śākyamuni's Teachings Newly Authorised in the Zhenyuan Era* (*Zhenyuan xinding shijiao mulu*, T55n2157_028), a Buddhist catalogue compiled by Monk Yuanzhao of the Monastery of Western Light (Ximing si) in 800 or the sixteenth year of the Zhenyuan era (785–805) during the reign of Emperor Dezong of the Tang dynasty. Indeed, there are so many of them that they amount to around one-third of the scriptures registered in the then Buddhist Canon (Zhang 2006: 23, quoted in Xiong 2015: 47).

---

1 A somewhat different yet more detailed account of the doubtful origin of this scripture appears later in the *Catalogue of Śākyamuni's Teachings Compiled in the Kaiyuan Era* (*Kaiyuan shijiao lu*, T55n2154_018.0675a01).

Another key term that merits an explanation here is 'translation'. There are two basic approaches to translation, that is, literal (word-for-word) translation and free (sense-for-sense) translation, the former being 'text-oriented' and the latter 'reader-oriented'. As mentioned above, I consider the *Yulanpen Sūtra* a creative translation rather than a Chinese Buddhist composition. By 'creative translation' is not simply meant 'free translation' but 'reader-oriented localisation'. Thus, the term 'creative translation' is used in this study to refer to the use of idiomatic, indigenous, idiosyncratic and sometimes culturally specific expressions in the target (Sinitic) language to translate conceptually equivalent expressions in the source (Indic) language, and accordingly, the term 'localisation' indicates the process of giving a translated text the look and feel of having been created specifically for a target readership, no matter what their language, culture or location is. In this sense, 'localisation' is different from 'sinicisation', which, as defined by Kenneth Ch'en (1973: 5), refers to the process of 'Chinese fashioning changes in the Indian ideas and practices' – a process of transformation and adaptation of Buddhism to Chinese culture and society.

Chapter 1

YULANPEN SŪTRA AND MAUDGALYĀYANA

The Yulanpen Festival, also known as the Middle-Primordial (Zhongyuan) Festival (*Zhongyuan jie*), the Hungry Ghost Festival (*egui jie*) or simply as the Ghost Festival (*guijie*) (Figures 1.1–1.3), has its scriptural origin in the *Yulanpen Sūtra Expounded by the Buddha* (*Fo shuo Yulanpen jing*, T16n0685), a Buddhist text in the *fangdeng* (lit. 'square and equal') or *vaipūlya* ('[works of] great extent') category of the Chinese Buddhist canon.

Figure 1.1 Dharma Master Wenyuan officiates at Yulanpen Ceremony on the fifteenth day of the seventh lunar month or 15 August 2019 in the Rebirth Parlour (Wangsheng tang) of the Jade Buddha Monastery (Yufo chansi) in Shanghai. Photo by the author.

Figure 1.2 Zhongyuan Ceremony held on the fourteenth day of the seventh lunar month or 21 August 2021 in front of the Abbey of Pure Yang (Qingyang guan), Zherong County, Fujian Province. Photo courtesy of Huang Yongfeng.

Figure 1.3 Photo of Zhu Bijie burning joss money as offerings to ghost ancestors in the courtyard of her house on the fourteenth day of the seventh month or 11 August 2022 during the Ghost Festival, Doubei Village, Fengting Town, Xianyou County, Fujian Province. Photo courtesy of Huang Yongfeng.

The *Yulanpen Sūtra*

This is a fairly short text of approximately 800 Chinese characters (Figure 1.4a–c) and is worth citing here in its entirety because it is crucial to our understanding of this Buddhist scripture as a creative translation from some Indic source(s) and

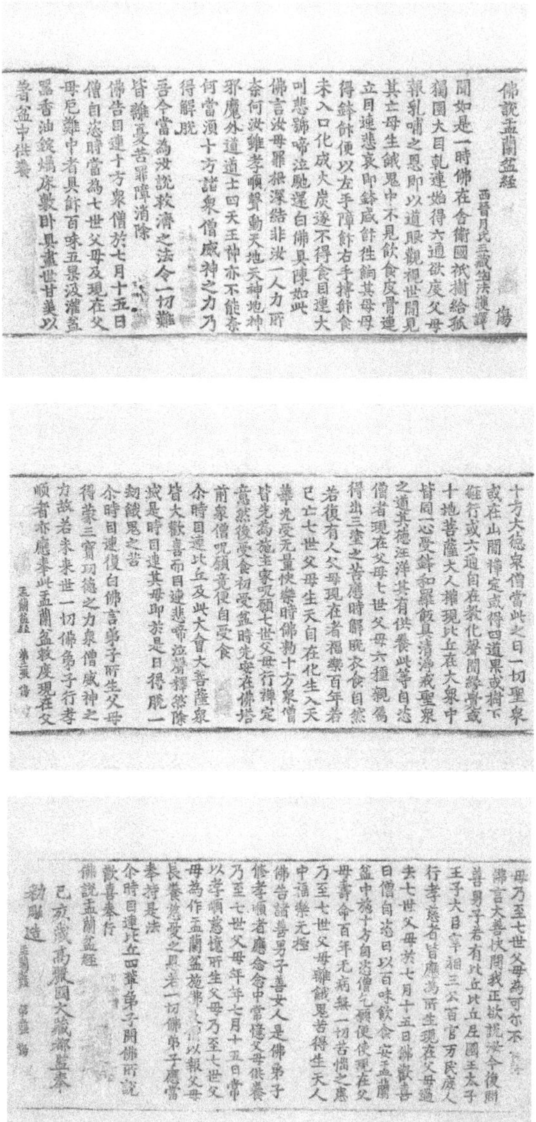

Figure 1.4a–c Korean woodblock print of *Yulanpen Sūtra Expounded by the Buddha* dated the year of Gihae (1239) and numbered K.0277 in the Goryeo Tripiṭaka or Palman Daejanggyeong (Eighty-Thousand Tripiṭaka). Image in the public domain.

also as the canonical source of the Yulanpen Festival that is still widely celebrated in China and beyond.

Yulanpen Sūtra Expounded by the Buddha
Translated into Chinese by Dharmarakṣa (Zhu Fahu),
Tripiṭaka Master from Gandhāra in the Western Jin Dynasty

Thus have I heard, at one time, the Buddha is dwelling in the Garden of the Benefactor of Orphans and the Solitary in the Jetavana Monastery in Śrāvastī when Maudgalyāyana had just obtained the six spiritual penetrations (*liutong*). He wished to deliver his parents from rebirth into a lower realm to repay their kindness for raising and nurturing him. Thus, he regarded the world with his divine eyes (*daoyan*) and found that his deceased mother had been reborn into the Preta realm. With nothing to eat or drink, she was but skin and bones.

Feeling deep pity and sadness, Maudgalyāyana filled a bowl with cooked rice and went forward to feed his mother. Having received the bowl, his mother screened it with her left hand while taking some rice with her right hand, but before the food entered her mouth, it turned into burning charcoal that could not be eaten. Maudgalyāyana cried out in agony and rushed back to the Buddha to tell him what had happened to his mother.

The Buddha said, 'Your mother's sins are so grave and deeply rooted that it is beyond your individual power to save her. Although your filial devotion and submission (*xiaoshun*) and your sound of crying have moved Heaven and Earth, there is nothing that heavenly gods, earthly deities, Māras (*xiemo*), non-Buddhist monks (*waidao*), Buddhist monks (*daoshi*) and the Four Great Heavenly Kings (Si tianwan shen) can do to save her. However, the supernatural power of the assembled Saṃgha of the Ten Directions shall be great enough to deliver her from the Preta realm. Now I shall preach to you the dharma of delivering all those in distress from worries and sufferings.'

The Buddha said to Maudgalyāyana, 'The fifteenth day of the seventh month is the Pavāraṇā Day (*zizi ri*) for the assembled Saṃgha of the Ten Directions. For the sake of your ancestors of seven generations (*qishi fumu*) and your present parents who are in distress, you should make an offering of bowls (*pen*) full of hundreds of flavours and the five fruits, vessels for drawing and pouring water, incense, oil, lamps, candles, beds and bedding, all the best of the world, to the greatly virtuous assembled Saṃgha of the Ten Directions. On that day, all the holy assembly – those who practice meditative concentration (*chanding*) in the mountains, those who have obtained the fourfold fruits, those who practice walking meditation beneath trees, those who edify disciples (*shengwen*) and solitary buddhas (*yuanjue*) by means of the six penetrations, or the Great Bodhisattvas Who Have Already Attained the Tenth Bhūmi (Shidi pusa) but provisionally manifest themselves as a bhikṣu – all in the great assembly shall receive the Pravāraṇa food with one mind. If one thus makes offerings to the Pravāraṇa Saṃghas, one's present parents and one's ancestors of past seven generations as well as one's six kinds of relatives (*liuqin*) will escape the suffering in the three paths (*santu*), attain salvation immediately from rebirth into a lower realm and will be clad and fed spontaneously. If one's parents are still alive, they will have wealth and blessings for a hundred years. If one's parents are deceased, [they as well as] one's ancestors of past seven generations will be reborn in Heaven. They will be reborn as they like and enter the light of celestial flowers and enjoy limitless bliss.'

At that time, the Buddha commanded the assembled Saṃgha of the Ten Directions to chant mantras and recite vows on behalf of the family of the donor for their ancestors of past seven generations. After practicing meditative concentration, the Saṃgha received the food with a settled mind. When they first accepted the bowl, they placed it before the Buddha in the stupa. When the assembled Saṃgha had finished chanting the mantras and reciting vows, they helped themselves to the food.

At that time, Bhikṣu Maudgalyāyana and the Assembly of Great Bodhisattvas all greatly rejoiced, and the sorrowful cries of Maudgalyāyana relievingly died out. Then, on that very day, Maudgalyāyana's mother obtained liberation from one kalpa (*jie*) of suffering in the Preta realm. Maudgalyāyana returned to the Buddha and said, 'Now the parents of your disciple are able to receive the power of the merit of the Triple Jewel thanks to the great spiritual power of the assembled Saṃgha. If in the future all disciples of the Buddha practice filial devotion and submission by offering up the *yulan* bowl (*yulanpen*), may they be able or not to deliver their present parents as well their ancestors of past seven generations?'

The Buddha replied, 'A very good question, indeed! This is just what I am about to preach. My good man, if bhikṣus, bhikṣunīs, kings, crown princes, ministers, chief ministers, the three ducal ministers (*sangong*), officials of all ranks (*baiguan*) and the tens of thousands of commoners all wish to practice compassionate filial piety (*cixiao*), for the sake of their present parents who bore them and their ancestors of past seven generations, on the fifteenth day of the seventh month, the Day of the Buddha's Delight (*Fo huanxi ri*), the Day of the Saṃgha's

Pravāraṇa (*zizi*), they all should place hundreds of flavours of foods in the yulanpen and offer them up to the Pravāraṇa Saṃgha of the Ten Directions. They should then request the Pravāraṇa Saṃgha to pray that their present parents live a hundred years without illnesses, sufferings, afflictions or worries and that their ancestors of seven generations be free from the suffering in the Preta realm, be reborn in the realm of Devas, and enjoy blessings and bliss without limit. The disciples of the Buddha who practice filial devotion and submission should constantly think of their present parents and their ancestors of up to seven generations. And every year, on the fifteenth day of the seventh month, they should, out of their filial devotion and compassion, think of their parents who bore them as well as their ancestors of up to seven generations and for their sakes, perform the offering of the yulanpen to the Buddha and the Saṃgha, thus repaying the compassionate love (*ci'ai*) of their parents who raised and nourished them. All the disciples of the Buddha should uphold this dharma.'

At that time, Bhikṣu Maudgalyāyana and the fourfold assembly of disciples rejoiced in the hearing of what the Buddha had preached and practiced it with delight.

Maudgalyāyana in Indian Buddhist Literature

Maudgalyāyana, the central character in the sūtra, was a well-documented historical figure – an older contemporary of Siddhārtha Gautama, the Buddha Śākyamuni. Also referred to by the honorific *mahā* as Mahāmaudgalyāyana (Damujianlian) in Buddhist texts, Maudgalyāyana was born to a Brahmin family in Kolita (Julütuo), a village near Rājagriha (Wangshecheng), the capital of the Kingdom of Magadha. He became a close friend of Śāriputra (Shelifu or Shelizi) from childhood. As recorded in the *Jākata* (*Bensheng jing*, N31n0018_001.0133a12), in their life-long pursuit of spiritual truth and nirvāṇa, Śāriputra and Maudgalyāyana first followed the teachings of the 'non-Buddhist' master Sañjaya Belaṭṭhiputta before being introduced to Śākyamuni Buddha who converted them to Buddhism and made them his two chief disciples (Figure 1.5). Both attained arhathood shortly after conversion to Buddhism.

Shortly afterwards, Maudgalyāyana attained the six penetrations (*liutong*) (*Fo shuo Yulanpen jing*, T16n0685_001.0779a28), namely the penetration of the celestial eye, the penetration of the celestial ear, the penetration of others' minds, the penetration of previous lives, the penetration of the spiritual realm and the penetration of the extinction of outflows, which are supernatural powers 'acquired through the persistent practice of meditative

Figure 1.5 Śākyamuni Buddha statue in centre flanked by statues of Maudgalyāyana on the left and Śāriputra on the right in the Main Hall of Yun Yang Temple, Melbourne, Australia. Photo courtesy of Monk Jason Tai.

concentration' (*Chengshi lun*, T32n1646_016.0369b11; see also *Yulanpen jing shu*, T39n1792_002.0507c22, quoted in Teiser 1988: 148–149). He is, therefore, frequently referred to as 'foremost in psychic power' or 'foremost in teleportation' in Buddhist literature such as the *Ekottarika āgama* (*Zengyi ahan jing*, T02n0125_029), the *Mahā prajñāpāramitā śāstra* (*Da zhidu lun*, T25n1509_011) and the *Sūtra on the Causes and Fruitions of the Past and Present* (*Guoqu xianzai yinguo jing*, T03n0189_004.0652c17).

Maudgalyāyana is also often portrayed as a good teacher and preacher in Indian Buddhist texts such as the *Kalpanā maṇḍitikā* (*Da zhuangyan lun jing*, T04n0201_007.0293b02), a collection of avadāna and jātaka tales attributed to Aśvaghoṣa (Ch. Maming), the brilliant second-century Sanskrit poet and playwright who adapted the conversion of Śariputra and Maugalyāyana to Buddhism into a nine-act drama, *Śāriputra prakaraṇa*, the earliest extant specimen of *prakaraṇa*, one of the ten types of Sanskrit drama in ancient India known as *daśarūpa*.

In Buddhist literature, particularly in its Theravāda tradition, there is a considerable number of tales about the previous lives of Maudgalyāyana across all the four (*deva-*, *mánusya-*, *tiryancha-* and *naraka-*) realms (*gatis*). Among the thirty-five previous lives of Maudgalyāyana recorded in Buddhist texts known to us, thirty are found in the *Jātaka* and two in *The Māra Tajjanīya Sutta* or *The Discourse on the Rebuking of Māra* (Tan 2011: 114–126), which has three Chinese versions, namely the *Scripture on the Subjugating of Māra* (*Xiangmo jing*) included in the *Madhyam āgama* (*Zhong ahan jing*, T01n0026_30.0620b09–0623a04), the *Scripture of Māra Testing Maudgalyāyana* (*Bimo shi Mulian jing*, T01n0067) and the *Scripture of Māra Assaulting* [*Maudgalyāyana*] (*Mo raoluan jing*, T01n0066), with the remaining four appearing, respectively, in the *Sūtra on the Omniscient Luminous Saints Who Possess the Causes and Conditions of Compassion in Not Eating Meat* (*Yiqie zhi guangming xianren cixin yinyuan bu shirou jing*, T03n0183_001.0458c19), the *Sūtra on the Wise and the Foolish* (*Xianyu jing*, T04n0202_008.0404b18–0409b24) and the *Principles and Precepts on Miscellaneous Matters of the Mūlasarvāstivāda School* or the *Mūlasarvāstivāda vinaya kṣudrakavastu* (*Genbenshuo yiqieyou bu pinaiye zashi*, T24n1451_018.0290b05–0290c09).[1]

It is worth noting that out of the thirty-five previous lives of Maudgalyāyana, seventeen are in the Tiryancha-gati as animals, birds, insects or plants, thirteen in the Mánuṣya-gati as human beings, four in the Deva-gati as celestial beings or demi-gods and one in the Naraka-gati as a ghost.[2] It is in *Māra Tajjanīya Sutta* that Maudgalyāyana manifests his three psychic powers (the divine eye, telepathy and recollection of past lives) all at once. And it is also only on this occasion that Maudgalyāyana reveals his own distant karmic past as Māra Dūsī, who is condemned to the Naraka-gati for having sinned against Krakucchaṃda Buddha, the fourth of the Seven Buddhas of Antiquity by attacking a chief disciple of the Buddha.

Conclusion

In the *Yulanpen Sūtra*, Maudgalyāyana or Mulian is portrayed as a devoted disciple of the Buddha, a filial son of a sinful mother, a spirit medium who communicates between the human world and the spirit world, and a *bhikṣu* (*biqiu*) or *śramaṇa* (*shamen*) who has just obtained the six penetrations. None of

1 A similar account of the karma story about Maudgalyāyana recorded in the *Mūlasarvāstivāda vinaya kṣudrakavastu* appears in the *Dhammapadaṭṭhakathā* – a commentary to the *Dhammapada* attributed to Buddhaghosa (fl. fifth century) – under the title of 'Death of Moggallāna the Great'. See Burlingame (2020) for an English translation of this story.

2 In his MA thesis on the images of Maudgalyāyana in Buddhist scriptures, Wang Chongming (2017: 3–40) lists a total of thirty-three previous lives of Mulian, but the list fails to include his rebirth into Naraka-gati described in *Māra Tajjanīya Sutta* and his reincarnation as a human son in the *Dhammapadaṭṭhakathā*, which will be discussed later in more detail in Chapter 4.

these attributes, however, is original to the *Yulanpen Sūtra*, as Teiser (1988: 114) notes. Rather, they all feature prominently in the *Discourses Increasing by One* or *Ekottarāgama* (*Zengyi ahan jing*, T02n0125_028-029; T02n0125_036), which was translated into Chinese by Gautama Saṃghadeva around AD 398. In this canonical Buddhist scripture, Mulian manifests himself as an invincible shaman who exercises his psychic powers of meditation, teleportation and therianthropy to travel through the universe and suppress the rebellions of nāgas. The six penetrations Mulian acquires through the persistent practice of trance-like deep spiritual meditation show a striking resemblance to *shentong* or 'spiritual penetration', a kind of supernatural power that a wu-shaman was widely believed to possess in early and medieval China.[3] The triple role of Mulian as a devout monk, as a filial son and particularly as a quintessential shaman accounts for the enormous popularity of the Mulian myth in China.

3 For an inspiring discussion of Mulian as a shaman, see Teiser (1988: 140–167).

Chapter 2

ETYMOLOGIES OF *YULAN*, *PEN* AND *YULANPEN*

Maudgalyāyana features prominently both as a filial son and as a devout monk in the *Yulanpen Sūtra*. This sūtra bears the compound word *yulanpen* in its title. The headword *pen* is a common noun in Chinese, meaning 'basin', 'vessel' or 'bowl', whereas its disyllabic dependent or modifier *yulan* does not make any sense in and of itself except understood as a transliteration of an Indic word that relates to the offering ritual performed on the fifteenth day of the seventh lunar month, but it is not clear as to what is exactly meant by *yulan* in its Indic origin because of lack of the original text(s) of the sūtra for reference.

Etymological Interpretations by Monk Scholars from Tang-Song China

Around the mid-seventh century, the Tang dynasty (618–907) monk scholar Xuanying (fl. 645) provided a detailed explanation of the word *yulanpen* in the *Sounds and Meanings of All Scriptures in the Buddhist Canon* (*Yiqie jing yinyi*, C056n1163_013):

> This word [*yulanpen*] is misleading. Its correct form is *wulanpona*, meaning 'hanging upside down' (*daoxuan*). As is the custom in the Western Country (Xiguo [i.e. India]), laypeople prepare abundant offerings and donate them to the Buddhist monks on the Day of the Saṃgha's Pravāraṇa in order for their deceased ancestors to be rescued from being suspended upside down. As a non-Buddhist book there says, 'If a deceased ancestor committed sins and if he has no descendants so that no one offers sacrifices to gods on his behalf or pleads with gods to save him, then he shall suffer the agony of being hung upside down in the realm of ghosts.' Although Buddhists there also follow the custom by performing the offering ritual, their purpose is to teach [laypeople] to sow the merits deep in the field of the Triple Jewel. The traditional interpretation of *yulanpen* as 'a vessel for the storage of food' (*zhushi zhi qi*) is thus incorrect.

Clearly, Monk Xuanying considers *yulanpen* or *wulanpona* not a native Chinese word but a transliteration of an Indic word or phrase, meaning 'hanging upside down'. He further points out that *wulanpona*, instead of meaning 'food vessel' as has been traditionally understood, refers to an ancient Indian custom – a form of ritual performed on the Pavāraṇā Day by both laypeople and Buddhists to save deceased ancestors from torture in Hell. Xuanying also cites a non-Buddhist (probably a pre-Buddhist) book as evidence for the origin of the Buddhist *wulanpona* ritual in the ancient Indian belief in karmic retribution and in the transference to the sinful ghost of the deceased ancestor the merits accumulated by his descendants through performing the ritual of offering sacrifices to gods for the sake of his rescue – a standard part of Buddhist spiritual discipline known as *pariṇāmanā* in Sanskrit and *pattidāna* or *pattānumodanā* in Pali.

Monk Xuanying's interpretation of *wulanpona* as 'hanging upside down' is accepted by Fayun (1088–1158), a Song dynasty (960–1279) monk-scholar who further interprets *wulanpona* as 'rescuing [somebody] from being hung upside down' (*jiu daoxuan*) in the *Collection of Translated Buddhist Terms* (*Fanyi mingyi ji*, T54n2131_004). Another Song dynasty monk-scholar, Yurong offers a more detailed explanation of the term in his sub-commentary on Zongmi's (780–841) *Commentary to the Yulanpen Sūtra* (*Yulanpen jing shu xiaoheng chao*, X21n0375_001.0519b10), saying:

> The sūtra is titled *Fotuo nishe wulanpona menzuoluo sudalan* [*sic*] in Sanskrit, which means in Chinese *Juezhe shuo jiu daoxuan qi jing* (*The Sūtra Expounded by the Enlightened One on the Vessel of Rescuing* [*Somebody*] *from Being Hung Upside Down*). [...,] hence the current title of *Fo shuo yulanpen jing* (*Yulanpen Sūtra Expounded by the Buddha*). The Sanskrit word 'Fotuo' simply means 'the Buddha', who is referred to here as Juezhe (the Enlightened One); [...,] the Sanskrit word for *shuo* ('to speak/ expound' is transliterated as *nishe* here. [...] As for *yulan pen*, according to the Great Song sūtra translator[s], it is a wrong abbreviation of a Sanskrit phrase. The correct reading [of *yulan*] is *wulanpona*, meaning 'filial devotion and submission' (*xiaoshun*), 'offering' (*gong*), 'compassion' (*en*) and 'hanging upside down' (*daoxuan*). The character *pen* is also a wrongly abbreviation of a Sanskrit word. The old reading is *penzuona*, and the new reading is *menzuoluo*, also *menzuonang*, which means in Chinese 'a vessel for rescue' (*jiuqi*). Thus, *yulan pen* should be taken to mean 'a vessel for recusing [those] from being hung upside down (*jiu daoxuan qi*)'.

Interestingly, Yurong thinks of *yulan pen* as a phrase rather than a compound word, interpreting the phrase as a 'wrong abbreviation' in transliteration of two Sanskrit words, that is, *wulanpona* and *menzuoluo*. He cites certain Song dynasty sūtra translator(s) as the source of information for his interpretation but stops short of naming them. Like their Tang dynasty predecessor Xuanying, both Fayun and Yurong fail to provide any evidence from Indic sources for their explanation, leaving behind the question of what the Indic form of *wulanpona*, *yulan*, *yulanpen*, *pen* or *menzuoluo* is.

Etymological Interpretations by Western and Japanese Scholars

There has since been much speculation and discussion as to the Indic form of *yulanpen* or *wulanpona* over the past two centuries (Ch'en 1968: 86–89; 1973: 61–64; Teiser 1988: 21–23). Stanislas Julien (1797–1873) made the first known attempt in modern Western scholarship to trace *wulanpona* to its Indic root. Based on the interpretations provided by Xuanying and Fayun, Julien (1861: 165) reconstructed *wulanpona* as *avalambana* but he did not give any evidence from Indic sources for his reconstruction, either. Ten years later, Ernst John Eitel (1838–1908), a German-born translator, lexicographer and missionary in China, published an important work titled *Handbook for the Student of Chinese Buddhism*, where he (1904: 185–186) proposed *ullambana* as the Indic form for the Chinese transliteration of *wulanpona*, followed by a fairly detailed account of the Chinese 'festival of all souls'. Although Eitel did not deny the influence of Confucian ancestor worship on the Ghost Festival, he (1904: 186) ascribed the origin of the Ghost Festival to the *Yulanpeng Sūtra*, stating:

> This agrees with the known fact that a native of Tukhâra, Dharmarakcha (A. D. 265–316), introduced in China and translated the Ullambana Sūtra 盂蘭盆經, which gives to the whole ceremonial the (forged) authority of Śâkyamuni and supports it by the alleged experiences of his principal disciples, Ānanda being said to have appeased Prêtas by food offerings presented to Buddha and Saṃgha, and Mâudgalyâyana to have brought back his mother who had been reborn in hell as a Prêta.

This was perhaps the first time that the *Yulanpen Sūtra* had been referred to as 'Ullambana Sūtra' in Western language publications. Shortly afterwards, Samuel Beal (1880: 86) published the first English translation of the scripture under the title of 'The Avalambana Sûtra'. In an explanatory note on his translation, Beal (1880: 85) expressed his objection to Eitel using *ulambana* instead of *avalambana* to render *yulanpen/wulanpona* for the reason as follows:

> This title *Ulamba* [*sic*] should doubtless be restored to *Avalambana*, as Julien gives it in his *Méthode* (1315), and as the Encyclopædia *Yi-tsi-kîng-yin-i* fully explains (*Kiwen* xiv., fol. 25). This title *Avalambana* seems to be derived from the idea of the suspension, head downwards, of the unhappy occupants of the *Limbus patrum*.

Beal cited Julien and Fayun to back up his objection without providing new evidence from either Chinese or Indic sources, so the original Indic form of *yulanpen* or *wulanpona* remains unclear.

In the *Catalogue of the Chinese Translation of Buddhist Tripiṭaka* compiled on the basis of the *Catalogue of the Chinese Buddhist Tripiṭaka* (*Daming Sanzang shengjiao mulu*), Bunyiu Nanjio (1883: 78) provided the hitherto most detailed explanation of *yulan* and *yulanpen*:

> The phrase 盂蘭 yü-lân in the Chinese title is generally understood as a transliteration of Ullambana, and translated by 倒懸 tâo-hhüen, "to hang upside down," or "to be in suspense." At the same time the character 盆 phan, "vessel," is explained as not a part of the transliteration. But this character may have been used here by the translator in both ways. On the one hand, it may stand for the last two syllables of Ullambana; on the other, it may mean the "vessel" of eatables to be offered to Buddha and Saṃgha for the benefit of those being in the Ullambana.

The Chinese word *yulanpen* or *wulanpona* has since been generally believed to be a transliteration of *ullambana*, but the problem is that there is no such word as *ullambana* in Sanskrit, although there are two Sanskrit words, namely *lambana* ('hanging down'; 'causing to hang down') or *avalamba* ('hanging down'; 'depending') that may be related to *ullambana*. Also noteworthy is the Pāli word *ullumpana* ('saving'; 'helping'), which is a noun derived from the verb *ullumpati* ('to take up'; 'to help'; 'to save'). It seems also likely that *yulanpen* or *wulanpona* is a transliteration of this Pāli word, as suggested by Karashima (2013b: 301–302), who traces the Indic origin of *yulan* to the Middle Indic form **olana* (<Skr. *odana*; Pāli: *Odana*, meaning 'boiled rice') and interprets *pen* as the headword in the compound *yulanpen*, meaning 'basin, bowl or vessel' as in the normal Chinese usage. Based on the possible etymological link between *yulan* and *olana*, Karashima (2013b: 301–302)

proposes that *yulanpen* should be understood as a compound consisting of the Indic *odana/Odana* and the Chinese native word *pen*, meaning 'a rice bowl', and accordingly, he believes that the Chinese title of the sūtra, *Yulanpen jing*, most probably means 'The Sūtra of Rice Bowl'.

It is also worth noting that another group of Japanese scholars trace the root of *yulanpen* to some Middle Iranian languages. For example, Imoto Eiichi (1966: 41–42, 92) believes the *yulanpen* has its origin in *ulavān māh*, a Middle Iranian form of *artavān māh*, 'a name of the Iranian first month of the year', whereas Iwamoto Yutaka (1968: 385–396; 1979: 225–231) considers that *yulanpen* is likely to have been derived from the Sogdian word *urvan*, meaning 'the soul [of the dead]'. Accordingly, they speculate that the Yulanpen Ceremony as described in the *Yulanpen Sūtra* is a Chinese Buddhist variant of the ancient cult of Central Asia.

Conclusion

So far, no consensus has been reached among scholars regarding the Indic or Iranian form(s) of the Chinese compound. However, most of them agree that *yulan*, *yulanpen* or *wulanpona* is not a native Chinese expression but a transliteration of an Indic or Iranian word that relates to the ritual performance of making offerings to the divine and/or the dead – with the notable exception of Xiong Juan (2014; 2015: 274–289), a Chinese palaeographer who argues that *yulan/lanpen/yulanpen* is not a Chinese transliteration but an indigenous Chinese word coined by means of 'phonetic borrowing'[1] alongside the composition of the *Yulanpen Sūtra* in China.

1 Phonetic borrowing (*jiajie*) is one of the Six Graphic Principles (*liushu*) in Chinese writing system under which a character is 'borrowed' to write another homophonous or near-homophonous morpheme.

Chapter 3

YULANPEN SŪTRA IN CHINESE BUDDHIST CATALOGUES

Tales about saving ghosts from suffering in Hell and about gaining rebirth in a better realm for oneself or for one's deceased ancestors by making merit through charitable acts are numerous in Buddhist scriptures, but none of them features Maudgalyāyana as the central character except the *Yulanpen Sūtra*.

Dharmarakṣa and Indian Buddhist Text Transmission and Translation in China

Traditionally, the Indo-Scythian Dharmarakṣa (aka Zhu Fahu, d. 308) is credited with the translation of the sūtra, although there is no such Buddhist scripture extant in any known Indic sources. Respectfully dubbed 'Bodhisattva Śramaṇa' (Pusa shamen) and 'Dunhuang Bodhisattva' (Dunhuang pusa), Dharmarakṣa was born and spent his childhood in Dunhuang, a major stop on the ancient Silk Road in northwestern China; he renounced the world and became a monk (*chujia*) at the age of eight and studied under Śrīmi (Shilimi), a Kuchean śramaṇa alternatively known as Gaozuo; during the reign period of Emperor Wu of Jin (Jin Wudi, r. 266–290), Dharmarakṣa travelled extensively with his Kuchean teacher across the Western Regions, studying local languages while searching for scriptures, and returned with a great number of Kharoṣṭhī texts (*huben*); and he lived most of his productive life in Luoyang and Chang'an (modern Xi'an), translating scriptures with the assistance of a team of Central Asian and Chinese bilingual śramaṇas and upāsakas, as noted by Monk Sengyou (445–518) in the 'Biography of Zhu Fahu' and elsewhere in the *Compilation of Notices on the Translation of the Tripiṭaka* (*Chu sanzang jiji*, T55n2145_013.0097c20; hereafter cited as *Sanzang jiji*; see also Mei 1996 and particularly Boucher 2006).[1]

---

1 Shortly afterwards, a large proportion of 'The Biography of Zhu Fahu' was incorporated verbatim by Huijiao (497–554) into his *Biographies of Eminent Monks* (*Gaoseng zhuan*, T50n2059_001.0326c02). For an annotated English translation of the biography in the *Compilation of Notices on the Translation of the Tripiṭaka*, see Boucher (2006: 14–21).

Dharmarakṣa was the most prolific Buddhist translator of the Western Jin (266–316). A total of 154 titles in 309 scrolls (*juan*) are listed in the *Compilation of Notices on the Translation of the Tripiṭaka* (*Sanzang jiji*, T55n2145_002.0007b08–0009b28) with Dharmarakṣa named as their translator. Of the 154 titles, sixty-four in a total of 116 scrolls are lost and known only by title to the compiler. Included now in the Taishō Tripiṭaka with Dharmarakṣa given as their translator are ninety-four titles, seventy-six of which are found listed in the *Compilation of Notices on the Translation of the Tripiṭaka*. As for the remaining eighteen titles, they are all credited to Dharmarakṣa as the translator in the Taishō Tripiṭaka probably under the influence of Chinese catalogues of Buddhist literature.

It must be pointed out, however, that Dharmarakṣa did not make the translation all on his own but for the most part through teamwork as was common practice among translators of Buddhist scriptures in early and medieval China (Boucher 2016: 35; Lung 2016: 112). Some of the colophons to his translated scriptures recorded in the *Compilation of Notices on the Translation of the Tripiṭaka* (*Sanzang jiji*, T55n2145_007) offer a vivid account of the normal process of his scriptural translation, from which we know that Dharmarakṣa usually 'recited a text aloud and orally delivered it in Chinese' (*kouxuan Jinyu*) for his Central Asian (Parthian, Kuchean and Sogdian) bilingual assistants such as An Wenhui, Kang Shu, Bo Yuanxin and Bo Faju to transcribe and transfer (*chuanyan*) to his Chinese scribes (notably Nie Chengyuan and his son Nie Daozhen), who 'would take them down in writing with a pen brush' (*bishou*).

These Indic texts come in two major types, texts written in the Brāhmī script (*fanben*) and texts in the Kharoṣṭhī script (*huben*), the former being the earliest known medium for writing Sanskrit and the latter an ancient Indo-Iranian script widely used in Gāndhārī and Central Asia (Boucher 2016: 26). Now it is impossible for us to tell for certain as to which of his translations was based on a Brāhmī text or a Kharoṣṭhī text because none of the original manuscripts brought back to China in the early period survive, but we have good reason to believe that most of the Indic source materials came from the Western Regions, Greater Gāndhārī in particular, where Dharmarakṣa travelled extensively in search of Buddhist scriptures when he was young. At the same time, we cannot exclude the possibility of a considerable number of his translations being based on oral texts retrieved from his memory rather than written texts carried back from the Western Regions. In actual fact, early Buddhist scriptural texts were 'designed' to facilitate their memorisation, recitation and oral (verbatim) transmission (Allon 1997a; 1997b; 2021; 2022), and their oral origin and transmission express themselves clearly in the stock opening phrase of sūtra, 'Thus have I heard' (Skr. *evaṃ mayā śrutam*; Ch. *ru shi wo wen*).

In a seminal article published in 1920 on the translation of Buddhist scriptures from ancient India, Liang Qichao (1999: 3795), a pioneering authority in modern scholarship on Chinese Buddhism, writes:

> Today, people would not think of translation without thinking of original texts written in a foreign language, which is read while held in hands before being rendered into Chinese. We are used to such kind of ideas about translation, believing that the translation of Buddhist scriptures has never been otherwise. It is not really the case, though. In the initial phases of Buddhist scriptural translation, there were hardly any written texts in the original available to their translators, who were thus left to resort to oral texts recited from memory. It is not that the translators would rather do without written copies in the original but that the original texts had not yet been written on bamboo and silk.

In Chinese context, the phrase 'bamboo and silk' (*zhubo*) is understood as a metaphorical reference to various types of material for writing before paper was invented during the Han dynasty (206 BC–AD 220). Liang is wrong here in saying that 'original texts had not yet been written on bamboo and silk' and he would have taken back his words if he had been aware of the use in ancient India of birch barks and palm leaves as media for writing scriptures, as evidenced by birch-bark and palm-leave scrolls dating from the first century AD and written in the Kharoṣṭhī script – the oldest known Buddhist manuscripts – that have recently been uncovered in Afghanistan and Pakistan (Allon 2008; Kornicki 2018: 218). That being said, his remarks about a general shortage of written copies of Buddhist texts in the transmission and translation of Buddhism in early medieval China are not sheer speculation but well founded.

In the *Records of Buddhist Kingdoms* (*Fuguo ji*), a travelogue alternatively titled *Biography of the Eminent Monk Faxian* (*Gaoseng Faxian zhuan*, T51n2085_001.0863a14), the Eastern Jin monk Faxian (ca. 337–422) notes:

> Faxian had planned to seek Buddhist precepts, and monastic rules and regulations (*jielü*). In the various states of North India, however, they were all orally transmitted among masters without written copies available for him to transcribe. Therefore, he travelled distantly into Central India.

In the *Treatise on Discerning Merits* (*Fenbie gongde lun*, T25n1507_002.0034a17), an early Chinese commentary on the *Collection of Texts Increasing by One* (*Ekottarika āgam*) written by a group of Chinese and Central Asian translators based on Indic source materials, we read:[2]

> Twelve years after the *Collection of Texts Increasing by One* came out, Ānanda entered nirvana. At that time, bhikṣus were all engaged in the practice of dhyana and no longer recited scriptures and reflected on them (*songxi*). Word went out among them that Buddhist karma (*ye*) was threefold with mental karma (*zuochan*) coming first, so they all gave up reading and reciting scriptures. After another twelve years, Bhikṣu Uttara also entered nirvana. From thenceforth, the *Collection* lost nine tenths of its text. Foreign masters transmitted the scripture orally to their disciples, and no written copy of the text is heard to have survived.

Yulanpen Sūtra in Chinese Buddhist Catalogues

Similar accounts of the loss and corruption of written texts in the course of their oral transmission are also found in the mid-fifth century *History of the Transmission of the Dharma-Storehouse* (*Fu Fazang yinyuan zhuan*, T50n2058_002.0302b25–0302c15) and also in an explanatory note offered by Monk Sengyou on the 'Catalogue of the Scriptures of Doubtful Authenticity Newly Collected by the Venerable [Dao']an)' ('Xinji Angong yijing lu') in his *Compilation of Notices on the Translation of the Tripiṭaka* (*Sanzang jiji*, T55n2145_005.0038b08).

Yulanpen Sūtra *in early medieval Chinese Buddhist catalogues*

The *Compilation of Notices on the Translation of the Tripiṭaka* is the earliest extant catalogue of Chinese Buddhist texts compiled during the Tianjian period (502–519) of the Liang dynasty, which, as noted by Sengyou, is largely an updated and expanded version of the now lost *Comprehensive Catalogue of the Scriptures* (*Zongli zhongjing mulu*), the earliest known catalogue of Chinese Buddhist texts compiled by the Eastern Jin monk Dao'an (314–385) (*Sanzang jiji*, T55n2145_002.0005b16). This is particularly the case with the list of the scriptures ascribed to Dharmarakṣa, to which Sengyou adds only four newly discovered texts in the *Compilation of Notices on the Translation of the Tripiṭaka* (*Sanzang jiji*, T55n2145_002.0009b28). Catalogued in the *Compilation of Notices on the Translation of the Tripiṭaka* (*Sanzang jiji*, T55n2145_004.0021b18)

2 The *Fenbie gongde lun* has been convincingly dated to AD 385 by Palumbo (2013: 179–265) in his book-length study of the date, authorship and authenticity of this Buddhist scripture in relation to the Chinese translation of the *Ekottarika āgama*.

is a one-scroll text titled *Yulan Sūtra* (*Yulan jing*), which, however, is not listed among those translated by Dharmarakṣa but grouped into 'anonymously translated miscellaneous scriptures' (*shiyi zajing*) together with the *Sūtra on Bathing the Buddha Image* (*Guanla jing*), the complete title of which is the *Sūtra on Bathing the Buddha Image after the Parinirvāna* (*Bannihuan hou guanla jing*, T12n0391).

The word *zajing*, literally meaning 'miscellaneous scripture', is an umbrella term used in Chinese Buddhist bibliography to refer to all Buddhist scriptures that do not fit well in with either the Mahāyāna tradition or the Theravāda tradition. 'Anonymously translated' (*shiyi*) as they are, both the *Yulan Sūtra* and the *Sūtra on Bathing the Buddha Image* are considered translations from Indic sources rather than indigenous creations, as neither of them is listed in the 'Catalogue of the Scriptures of Doubtful Authenticity Newly Collected by the Venerable [Dao']an)' or in the 'Miscellaneous Catalogue of Newly Collected Doubtful Scriptures and Spurious Texts' ('Xinji yijing weizhuan zalu') in the *Compilation of Notices on the Translation of the Tripiṭaka* (*Sanzang jiji*, T55n2145_005.0038b08–c16; 005.0038c–0039b13). The cataloguing in the history of Chinese Buddhist bibliography of 'doubtful scriptures' (*yijing*) and 'spurious scriptures' (*weijing*) begins with Dao'an's (314–385) *Comprehensive Catalogue of the Scriptures*, followed by Sengyou's (445–518) *Compilation of Notices on the Translation of the Tripiṭaka*, the former listing twenty-six titles in thirty scrolls, the latter twenty titles in twenty-six scrolls, totalling forty-six titles in fifty-six scrolls. Judging from the scope of their coverage, these listings seem to have included all apocryphal texts produced in China over the span of three hundred years from the late Eastern Han (AD 25–220) to the early Liang period (502–557).[3]

It seems that the *Yulan Sūtra* appeared no later than the mid-fourth century and continued to exist through the early sixth century when Sengyou compiled the catalogue of Buddhist scriptures based on the fourth-century *Comprehensive Catalogue of the Scriptures.* There is confusion, however, as to the relation of the 'anonymously translated' *Yulan Sūtra* to what later came to be known as the *Yulanpen Sūtra*, which is commonly ascribed to Dharmarakṣa as its translator in later catalogues of Chinese Buddhist scriptures. Born in 312, only four years after the death of Dharmarakṣa in 308, Monk Dao'an was acclaimed as the most erudite Buddhist scholar of his time by Monk Huijiao in the *Biographies of Eminent Monks* (*Gaoseng zhuan*, T50n2059_005.0351c03), so it is unlikely that Dao'an was completely unaware or ignorant of Dharmarakṣa having translated the *Yulanpen Sūtra*

3 For more about Dao'an and Sengyou's catalogues of doubtful and spurious scriptures, see Tokuno (1990: 33–40) and Makita (1985: 287–295).

into Chinese. Monk Sengyou was also well versed in Buddhist scriptures. He spent more than forty years searching for and sorting out Buddhist texts and set up sūtra repositories in the monasteries of Jianchu and Dinglin in Jianye (aka Jiankang, present-day Nanjing) – the first sūtra libraries ever built in Buddhist monasteries in China – for the sheer volume of sacred writings collected by him during the Tianjian period of the Liang dynasty when he was engaged in the compilation of the catalogue of Buddhist scriptures (*Gaoseng zhuan*, T50n2059_011.0402c04; see also *Sanzang jiji*, T55n2145_012.0087a16–0094c03), so it is not likely, either, that Sengyou was completely unaware or ignorant of the existence of a scripture under the title of *Yulanpen Sūtra* translated by Dharmarakṣa.

Thus, three possibilities exist with regards to the *Yulan Sūtra*/*Yulanpen Sūtra*: (1) the *Yulan Sūtra* and *Yulanpen Sūtra* are one and the same with the latter renamed from the former; (2) they are two different scriptures that have one common Indic origin; and (3) they are two different translations of one and the same Buddhist scripture. Anyway, that Monk Sengyou makes no mention of the *Yulanpen Sūtra* and that he labels the *Yulan Sūtra* as an 'anonymously translated scripture' cannot but call into question the ascription of the *Yulanpen Sūtra* to Dharmarakṣa as its translator even if it were renamed from *Yulan Sūtra*.

Yulanpen Sūtra *in late medieval Chinese Buddhist catalogues*

The first ever recorded ascription of the *Yulan Sūtra* to Dharmarakṣa as its translator appears in the *Records of the Triple Jewel Throughout the Successive Dynasties* (*Lidai sanbao ji*, T49n2034; hereafter cited as *Sanbao ji*), a catalogue and chronology of Chinese Buddhism completed in 598 by the Sui dynasty (581–618) Buddhist scholar Fei Changfang.[4] He provides a list of 210 titles in a total of 394 scrolls giving Dharmarakṣa as their translator (*Sanbao ji*, T49n2034_006.0061c11–0064c14). Among them is a one-scroll text titled *Yulan jing* or *Yulan Sūtra* (*Sanbao ji*, T49n2034_006.0064a27). The first known bibliographic record of the *Yulanpen Sūtra* is also found in the *Records of the Triple Jewel Throughout the Successive Dynasties*, where the *Yulanpen Sūtra* is listed separately from the *Yulan Sūtra* as one of the 316 titles in the 'Catalogue of Anonymously Translated Hīnayāna Sūtras' ('Xiaocheng xiuduoluo shiyi lu') (*Sanbao ji*, T49n2034_014.0116c06–0119a27) and grouped together with the *Sūtra on Bathing the Buddha Image* and the *Sūtra on Offering Bowls to Repay Kindness*

4 For an informative study of the role of the *Records of the Three Treasures Throughout the Successive Dynasties* in the formation of the Chinese Buddhist canon, see Storch (2015).

(*Bao'en fengpen jing*) as 'three scriptures that were each summarily translated under a different title from one common original text' (*sanjing tongben bieyi yiming*) (*Sanbao ji*, T49n2034_014.0118c11–0118c12). The ascription of the translation of the *Yulan Sūtra* to Dharmarakṣa and the categorisation of the *Yulanpen Sūtra* as a summary translation of one and the same unnamed Indic text as the two otherwise titled Buddhist scriptures, as we have seen in the *Records of the Triple Jewel Throughout the Successive Dynasties*, cannot but cause greater confusion as to whether the *Yulan Sūtra* with Dharmarakṣa named as its translator is one and the same as the *Yulanpen Sūtra* that is listed in the 'Catalogue of Anonymously Translated Hīnayāna Sūtras' separately from the *Yulan Sūtra*.

Apart from the *Records of the Triple Jewel Throughout the Successive Dynasties*, the short-lived Sui dynasty (581–618) also witnesses the compilation of two official catalogues of Buddhist texts under the same title, namely the *Catalogue of Collected Scriptures* (*Zhongjing mulu*). The first *Catalogue of Collected Scriptures* was compiled in 594 or the fourteenth year of Kaihuang (581–600) during the Tang dynasty (618–907) at the Monastery of the Great Propagation of Goodness (Daxingshan si) by Monk Fajing and others (*Xu gaoseng zhuan*, T50n2060_002.0433b12; *Zhongjing mulu*, T55n2146) and the second in 602 or the second year of Renshou by a group of monk translators and scholars headed by Yancong (557–610) (*Xu gaoseng zhuan*, T50n2060_002.0433b15; *Zhongjing mulu*, T55n2147), a disciple of Monk Xuanzang (602–664), the greatest Chinese translator of Buddhist scriptures. Surprisingly, the *Yulan Sūtra* makes no appearance in either of the two official Buddhist catalogues, whereas the *Yulanpen Sūtra* is found listed alongside the *Sūtra on Bathing the Buddha Image* and the *Sūtra on Offering Bowls to Repay Kindness* as 'three scriptures translated from one common original text but listed separately from one another' (*sanjing tongben chongchu*) in the section of 'Anonymously Translated Scriptures' ('Zhongjing shiyi') of the Kaihuang catalogue (*Zhongjing mulu*, T55n2146_003.0133b12) and as 'three different translations of one common original text' (*sanjing tongben yiyi*) in the section of 'Hīnayāna Scriptures with More than One Translation' ('Xiaocheng jing chongfan') of the Renshou catalogue (*Zhongjing mulu*, T55n2147_002.0160a21).

Commissioned – eight years apart – by the Imperial Court, the two Sui official Buddhist catalogues enjoy a good reputation among scholars of Chinese Buddhism, and the Renshou catalogue, in particular, is hailed as 'a reliable and valuable source for investigating the currency of texts during the Sui' for its careful differentiation of extant from non-extant (Tokuno 1990: 40). Now we are able to say with somewhat reasonable certainty that the text titled *Yulan jing* or *Yulan Sūtra* failed to exist beyond the sixth century, although it remains hitherto unclear as to whether the *Yulan Sūtra* survived and continued to exist under a new title, that is, *Yulanpen jing* or *Yulanpen Sūtra*.

Although we are still unable to pinpoint at this stage exactly as to what kind of textual relationship there might be between the *Yulan Sūtra* and the *Yulanpen Sūtra*, the three sūtras (the *Yulanpen Sūtra*, the *Sūtra on Bathing the Buddha Image* and the *Sūtra on Offering Bowls to Repay Kindness*) that are listed in all the three Sui catalogues of Buddhist scriptures are undeniably related to each other, as confirmed by the *Catalogue of the Inner Canon of the Great Tang* (*Da Tang neidian lu*, T55n2149; hereafter cited as *Da Tang lu*), compiled in 664 by Monk Daoxuan (596–667) for his newly established library at the Monastery of Western Light (Ximing si). In Scroll Seven under the heading of 'Record of Hīnayāna Scriptures, Extant and Non-extant, with One or More Translations' ('Xiaocheng jing dan chong fan ben bing yi youwu lu'), the Great Tang catalogue lists the *Yulanpen Sūtra*, the *Sūtra on Bathing the Buddha Image* and the *Sūtra on Offering Bowls to Repay Kindness* as 'three scriptures that are separately translated from one common original text' (*sanjing tongben yichu*) without naming their translator(s) (*Da Tang lu*, T55n2149_007. 0298b08–0298b19), although they are all sorted into the 'Register of Canonical Texts' ('Ruzang lu') under the sub-heading of 'Hīnayāna Scriptures with More Than One Translation' (*Da Tang lu*, T55n2149_008.0309a20–0310b02). This is unusual, as titles listed in Scroll Seven are mostly followed by the name of their translator (*Da Tang lu*, T55n2149_007.0296a22–0302b12). The only possible explanation we may come up with is that Monk Daoxuan does not know for certain who did the translation, although Dharmarakṣa is named as the translator of *Yulan Sūtra* in the several earlier catalogues of Chinese Buddhist scriptures. Notwithstanding, the *Yulanpen Sūtra* is singled out in the *Catalogue of the Inner Canon of the Great Tang* from among the variant versions of Yulan scriptures as the most 'appropriate for recitation' (*zhuandu*) (*Da Tang lu*, T55n2149_009.0322c02) and has since become a primary source of information and inspiration for the Mulian myth and Mulian performance in China (Zhao 2021a; Zhao 2021b).

It is worth mentioning that under the entry of the *Yulanpen Sūtra* in the Great Tang catalogue, Monk Daoxuan notes the existence of a five-sheet (*ye*) text titled *Pure Land Yulanpen Sūtra* (*Jingtu Yulanpen jing*) as a 'variant version' (*bieben*) of the *Yulanpen Sūtra*, but he excludes it from the 'Register of Canonical Texts' because he 'does not know whence it is translated' (*Da Tang lu*, T55n2149_007.0298b19). Despite its enormous popularity with the common people during the Tang dynasty, the *Pure Land Yulanpen Sūtra* has never been accepted into the Chinese Buddhist canon mainly because of its dubious origin as noted in the 730 *Catalogue of Śākyamuni's Teachings Compiled in the Kaiyuan Era* (*Kaiyuan shijiao lu*, T55n2154_018.0672a01; hereafter cited as *Kaiyuan lu*) and maybe also because of its vulgar narrative style and impious language and of its description of extravagant and imprudent offerings by the ruling elites (Teiser 1988: 58).

This Pure Land scripture seems to have failed to survive in its entirety beyond the eighth century. A small part of this text is cited under the title of *Pure Land Sūtra of the Large Bowl* (*Dapen jingtu jing*) in the *Pearl Grove in the Dharma Garden* (*Fayuan zhulin*, T53n2122_0062.0751a03–0751a13), a Tang dynasty Buddhist encyclopaedia completed around the year of 668 by Monk Daoshi (d. 683), and also in the *Six Books of the Śākya Clan* (*Shishi liutie*, B13n0079_022.0461a06), a Five Dynasties (907–960) Buddhist encyclopaedia compiled by Monk Yichu. A hand-copied text with the same title, recovered in Dunhuang in the early twentieth century, now included and numbered 2,185 in the Pelliot Collection, has a length of approximately 1,800 characters written in 120 vertical lines on five sheets of paper (Figure 3.1).

Significantly, the *Pure Land Yulanpen Sūtra* offers at its end a fairly detailed description of the previous lives of Mulian and his mother in the era of the Dīpankara Buddha (Dingguangfo) as an explanation for the 'causal condition' (*yinyuan*) of their reincarnation and situation in their present lives. Notably, there are also references in this Pure Land text to two prominent lay disciples and protectors of the Buddha, Bimbisāra (Pinshawang, ca. 558–ca. 491 BC) and Prasenajit (Bosiliwang, fl. mid-sixth century), which is viewed as evidence by some scholars (e.g. Chen 1999: 243) for the existence in Indian Buddhist literature of some different version of the story of Mulian saving his mother.

Before becoming a monk, as related in the *Pure Land Yulanpen Sūtra*, Mulian was a devout and dutiful young man named Luobo and Qingti was his mother.

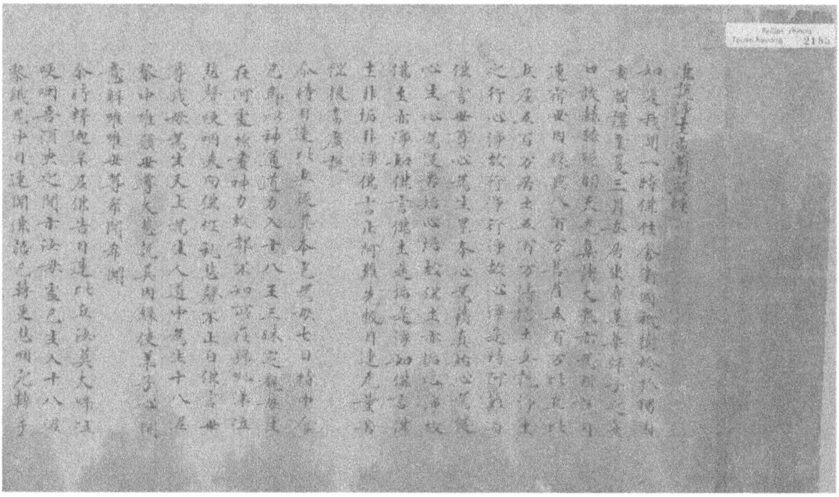

Figure 3.1 Hand-written copy of *Pure Land Yulanpen Sūtra*.

Source: Bibliothèque nationale de France. Département des Manuscrits. Pelliot chinois 2,185. Image in the public domain.

Noteworthy is the Chinese word *luobo* ('white radish'), which is a familiar name for simple, solid and steady young men and also a common name for Raphanus sativus (*laifu*; *luofu*). Aside from Mulian, Mujianlian, Damujianlian, Mohemujianlian, Muganlian, Damuganlian and Mohemuganlian, Maudgalyāyana is also called in Chinese Laifu, Luofu, Laifugen or Luofugen ('White Radish Root') probably to suggest his filial affection for parents because the white radish root is a favourite dish of his father according to a parenthetical note on Damujianlian in the *Sūtra on the Questions of Mañjuśrî* (*Wenshushili wen jing*, T14n0468_001.0492c02).[5]

And so the text continues. One day, Luobo went on a business trip, asking his mother to give alms to beggars and itinerant monks during his absence. However, Qingti gave no offerings to almsmen but instead deceived his son into believing that she had given food, water and accommodation to the poor and needy. As a result, she was reborn into the Preta realm as a hungry ghost, enduring terrible pain and suffering that no one could relieve except through the *yulanpen* offering. This is the first known reference in Chinese literary sources to Luobo as Mulian's secular name and Qingti as his mother, of which no mention whatsoever is made in Chinese Buddhist canonical texts except in a brief explanatory note made in the *Commentary to the Yulanpen Sūtra* (*Yulanpen jing shu*, T39n1792_002.0506c20) by the Tang dynasty Chan master Zongmi (784–841), who, however, cites a certain unnamed scripture (*you jing zhong shuo*) instead of giving the uncanonical *Pure Land Yulanpen Sūtra* as the source for his note. This avadāna tale later finds its way into the Tang dynasty vernacular and prosimetric narratives, 'popular sūtra lectures' (*sujiang*) and 'transformation texts' (*bianwen*) (Zhao 2021b) and has since become an integral part of the myth of Mulian rescuing his mother in China. Uncanonical as it is, this Pure Land text marks a key intermediary stage in the development of the Mulian myth from canonical Buddhist scriptures to popular prosimetric performances (Teiser 1988: 61).

Neither the *Pure Land Yulanpen Sūtra* nor the *Yulan Sūtra* is included in the *Collated Catalogue of Collected Scriptures Compiled in the Great Zhou* (*Da Zhou kanding zhongjing mulu*, T55n2153; hereafter cited as *Da Zhou mulu*). Compiled in the year 695 under the aegis of Empress Wu Zetian (r. 684–704) by a group of seventy monks led by Mingquan, the Great Zhou catalogue lists the *Yulanpen Sūtra*, the *Sūtra on Bathing the Buddha Image* and the *Sūtra on Offering Bowls to Repay Kindness* together as 'three scriptures translated from one common original text but listed separately from

5 Mair (1983: 224–225) believes that Luobo as a nickname by which Mulian is also known in China results from the confusion of Mulian – a Chinese abbreviated transliteration of Maudgalyāyana – with the Sanskrit word *Mūram* or *Mūlam* for 'turnip'.

one another' (*Da Zhou mulu*, T55n2153_009.0431c06–0431c10), as they are in the Kaihuang catalogue (*Zhongjing mulu*, T55n2146_003.0133b12). Notably, however, the Great Zhou catalogue names Dharmarakṣa as the translator of the *Yulanpen Sūtra* and the *Sūtra on Bathing the Buddha Image* without mentioning the translator of the *Sūtra on Offering Bowls to Repay Kindness*, giving the Sui dynasty Buddhist scholar Fei Changfang as the source for cataloguing these three Yulan scriptures, notwithstanding that they are described as 'anonymously translated scriptures of Hīnayāna Buddhism' in the received text of Fei's *Records of the Triple Jewel Throughout the Successive Dynasties* (*Sanbao ji*, T49n2034_014.0116c06–0119a27). The earlier Great Tang catalogue makes no mention of the translator(s) of the three Yulan texts, either, which makes the Great Zhou catalogue the first Chinese Buddhist catalogue to ascribe the translation of the *Yulanpen Sūtra* to Dharmarakṣa.

Following the Great Zhou catalogue, the *Catalogue of Śākyamuni's Teachings Compiled in the Kaiyuan Era* lists the *Yulanpen Sūtra* among 175 titles in a total of 354 scrolls attributed to Dharmarakṣa as their translator, describing it as a 'one-scroll text, which is known alternatively as *Yulan Sūtra* and which shares the same origin with the *Sūtra on Offering Bowls to Repay Kindness*' (*Kaiyuan lu*, T55n2154_00 2.0495b05). This is the first time for the *Yulanpen Sūtra* to be identified as the *Yulan Sūtra* in Chinese Buddhist bibliography, although they have been catalogued separately from each other as two seemingly different texts since the late sixth-century *Records of the Triple Jewel Throughout the Successive Dynasties.* Compiled single-handedly by Monk Zhisheng of the Western Monastery of the Exaltation of Blessings (Xi chongfu si) in Chang'an, the Kaiyuan catalogue was adopted as an official catalogue shortly after its completion in the eighteenth year (730) of the Kaiyuan era (713–741) in the early reign of Emperor Xuanzong (r. 712–756) of the Tang dynasty. Its 'Register of Canonical Texts', which contains 1,076 (Mahāyāna and Hīnayāna) titles in a total of 5,048 scrolls, serves as the standard for the Tang Buddhist canon and has since become a model for all successive Buddhist canons compiled in China, Korea and Japan, including the Taishō Tripiṭaka.

The ascription of the *Yulanpen Sūtra* to Dharmarakṣa as the translator in the Great Zhou and Kaiyuan catalogues is confirmed in the *Catalogue of the Śākyamuni's Teachings Newly Authorised in the Zhenyuan Era* (*Zhenyuan xinding shijiao mulu*, hereafter cited as *Zhenyuan mulu*), an imperially authorised Buddhist catalogue compiled by Monk Yuanzhao of the Monastery of Western Light in 800 or the sixteenth year of the Zhenyuan era (785–805) during the reign of Emperor Dezong (r. 779–805) of the Tang dynasty (*Zhenyuan mulu* T55n2157_001.0771a19–0771a21). Notably, the *Yulanpen Sūtra* is placed alongside the *Sūtra on Offering Bowls to Repay Kindness* as 'two scriptures differently translated from one common original text' (*erjing tongben yiyi*) among the 'Scriptures with Multiple Translations beyond the Five Great Divisions ('Wudabu wai zhu chongyi jing') in the Zhenyuan catalogue (T55n2157_021.0928a14–0928a18), whereas the *Sūtra on Bathing the Buddha Image after the Parinirvāna* is listed in the 'Section of Mahāyāna Scriptures with Only One Translation' ('Dacheng jing danyi') as translated by Dharmarakṣa from an original text different from that for the *Yulanpen Sūtra* and the *Sūtra on Bathing the Buddha* (*Zhenyuan mulu*, T55n2157_022.0938a28), although all the three scriptures are included in the 'Register of Canonical Texts' (T55n2157_029).

The most detailed explanation from medieval China of the translation of the *Yulanpen Sūtra* in relation to that of the *Sūtra on Bathing the Buddha Image* and *Sūtra on Offering Bowls to Repay Kindness* appears in the *Commentary to the Yulanpen Sūtra* (*Yulanpen jing shu*, T39n1792_00 2.0506c20) by the Tang dynasty Chan master Zongmi, who notes:

> There are three translations of this scripture, one translated under the title of *Yulanpen Sūtra* by Master Dharmarakṣa during the reign of Emperor Wu [r. 265–290] of the Jin dynasty, one under the title of *Sūtra on Bathing the Buddha Image* by Master Faju[6] during the reign of Emperor Hui [r. 290–307] of the Jin dynasty, and one under the title of *Sūtra on Offering Bowls to Repay Kindness* by a certain unnamed master.

Like his predecessors, however, Monk Zongmi does not provide any evidence for ascribing the translation of the *Yulanpen Sūtra* to Dharmarakṣa, either, nor does he provide any evidence for crediting Monk Faju with the translation of the *Sūtra on Bathing the Buddha Image*, thus leaving open the possibility that the *Yulan Sūtra*/*Yulanpen Sūtra* is a Chinese indigenous Buddhist scripture rather than a translation by Dharmarakṣa from some Indic source(s).

Apart from the *Yulanpen Sūtra* and the *Pure Land Yulanpen Sūtra*, the Mulian myth also finds expression in the *Sūtra on Bathing the Buddha Image* and the *Sūtra on Offering Bowls to Repay Kindness*. The received text of *Sūtra on Bathing the Buddha Image* (*Guanla jing*, T12n0391) is a short scripture of 428 characters about the ritual of bathing the Buddha image (*guan*) with fragrant water

6 In his study of 'Dharmarakṣa and the Transmission of Buddhism to China', Boucher (2006: 21) expresses his suspicion that this Faju is none other than Bo Faju, 'who is recorded to have served as a scribe (*bishou* 筆受) on Dharmarakṣa's translation of the *Lalitavistara* in 308', and he quotes Monk Sengyou as saying: 'It is not known whence he came. He translated *Loutan jing* 樓炭經 (**Lokasthāna-suūtra*). [Fa]ju and the *śramaṇa* Fali 法立 together translated two *sū tras*: *Fajuyu* 法句喻 (*Dharmapada*) and *Futian* 福田 (*Sū tra on the Fields of Merit*)'.

and also about the ritual of offering sacrifices (*la*) – food placed in bowls – to the Buddha and the Saṃgha on the fifteenth day of the seventh month in order for one's ancestors of past seven generations and six kinds of relatives to be released from suffering in Hell. The anonymously translated *Sūtra on Offering Bowls to Repay Kindness* (*Fengpen jing*, T16n0686) is an even shorter text of 328 characters, less than half of the length of the *Yulanpen Sūtra*. Datable to the Eastern Jin dynasty (317–420), the *Sūtra on Offering Bowls to Repay Kindness* reads like a summary of the *Yulanpen Sūtra*[7] and may have been a summary translation of an unknown Indic text from which the longer *Yulanpen Sūtra* was also translated, as noted by Fei Changfang in the *Records of the Triple Jewel Throughout the Successive Dynasties* (*Sanbao ji*, T49n2034_014.0118c11–0118c12). Besides, the Mulian myth also appears under the entry of 'Mulian Makes a Basin for His Mother' ('Mulian weimu zaopen'), a short passage quoted in the *Differentiated Manifestations of the Sūtra and Vinaya Piṭaka* (*Jinglü yixiang*, T53n2121_014.0073c22), a sixth-century Chinese Buddhist encyclopaedia compiled by Monk Baochang (ca. 495–528), Sengmin (427–527) and others, who give the *Yulan Sūtra* as the source for the entry.

Conclusion

Chinese Buddhist texts began to be systematically catalogued in the Eastern Jin dynasty when there appeared the first known Buddhist catalogue titled *Comprehensive Catalogue of the Scriptures* (*Zongli zhongjing mulu*) compiled by Master Dao'an (314–385). Over four hundred years from the Eastern Jin to the Zhenyuan era of the Tang dynasty, ten Buddhist catalogues were produced, and nine of them contain sections on apocryphal scriptures, which total 423 (Wang 1997: 3–24), but none of them have the *Yulanpen Sūtra* listed as a spurious scripture or a doubtful scripture, although they differ from one another in viewing the *Yulanpen Sūtra* in relation to the *Sūtra on Bathing the Buddha Image* and the *Sūtra on Offering Bowls to Repay Kindness*.

Now it is clear that the *Yulanpen Sūtra* was alternatively known as the *Yulan Sūtra* in medieval China. It is also clear that the *Yulanpen Sūtra/Yulan Sūtra*, albeit once listed as 'anonymously translated', has been consistently treated in Chinese Buddhist catalogues as an authentic text translated from an Indic original text and thus 'admitted to the Buddhist canon' (*ruzang*). It remains, however, inconclusive as to whether the scripture was translated by the Indo-Scythian Dharmarakṣa.

---

7 For a parallel English translation of the *Yulanpen Sūtra* and the *Sūtra on Offerings Bowls to Repay Kindness* and a brief comment on the similarities and differences between these two texts, see Teiser (1988: 49–54).

Chapter 4

YULANPEN SŪTRA: APOCRYPHAL OR AUTHENTIC?

Although the *Yulanpen Sūtra* is widely considered to be the primary source for the Mulian myth, the origin of this sūtra has been the subject for much debate and discussion among scholars of Chinese religion since the mid-twentieth century. There is no extant such scripture in Indic sources known to us, nor is there any mention in them of Maudgalyāyana's journeys to the Dark Regions to rescue his mother (Bandō 2005; Kapstein 2007). The dearth of direct textual evidence in Indic sources and the centuries-long confusion and controversy surrounding the translation, transmission and cataloguing of the *Yulan Sūtra*/*Yulanpen Sūtra* as examined in the previous chapter have cast doubt on the authenticity of this Buddhist scripture. Little wonder that the *Yulanpen Sūtra* is frequently regarded as a Chinese Buddhist apocryphal scripture as shown in Ikeda (1926: 59–64), Honda (1927), Fujino (1956: 340–345), Iwamoto (1968; 1979: 10–20), Miyakawa (1973: 225), Makita (1976: 47–50, 84), Chen (1983: 1–2), Mair (1989: 17), Irisawa (1990: 152), Zhu (1987: 54–59; 1993: 3–11), Teiser (1986: 48–49; 1988: 46;[1] 1989: 192), Liao (1995: 5–6), Hsiao (1995: 231–296; 1996: 83–98; 2005: 326–333), Yin (2006: 17–19), Yoshikawa (2003: 62), Tsuchiya (2005: 189–191) and Xiong (2014; 2015: 247–289), to name but a few.[2] Most representative of them are perhaps Iwamoto, Zhu and Hsiao.

---

1 While viewing the *Yulanpen Sūtra* alongside the *Sūtra on Offering Bowls to Repay Kindness* (*Bao'en fengpen jing*, T16n0686) and the *Pure Land Yulanpen Sūtra* (*Jingtu yulanpen jing*, Pelliot MS no. 2185) as 'three canonical and apocryphal sūtras' that 'were recorded (probably written) in China between the fifth and seventh centuries', Teiser (1986: 48–49) also draws attention to Ogawa's (1973: 159–171) thesis that the *Yulanpen Sūtra* 'grew out of the Dharmagupta sect in northwest India, ca. 400'.

2 For a useful summary of modern scholarship, particularly Japanese language scholarship, on the *Yulanpen Sūtra*, see Xiong (2014: 86–88) and especially Wu (2001: 6–10, 15–19).

Major Arguments against the Authenticity of the Text

Iwamoto was one of the first major Japanese scholars to challenge the authenticity of the *Yulanpen Sūtra*. He (1968, quoted in Zhu 1993: 8; 1979: 9ff.) claims that the sūtra is not a translation from India, let alone a translation by Dharmarakṣa, mainly on the grounds that:

(1) The content of the Mulian story is not found elsewhere in sources from ancient India;
(2) The 'divine eye' (Skr. *divyacakṣus*; Ch. *tianyan*) is a common expression in Indian Buddhist texts, whereas the 'eye of the Way' (*daoyan*) that occurs in the *Yulanpen Sūtra* is a typical Chinese indigenous expression;
(3) The conception of 'filial devotion and submission' (*xiaoshun*) is peculiar to Chinese lineage culture, as is the conception of 'six kinds of relatives' (*liuqin*) that finds no equivalent in Indian Buddhist texts, where the odd number 'five' or 'seven' tends to be used to refer to types of relatives;
(4) And this scripture begins with the phrase *wen ru shi* or 'What was heard was thus', thus distinguishing itself from authentic scriptures translated from Indian Buddhist sūtras which usually begin with the opening formula *ru shi wo wen* or 'Thus have I heard'.

Zhu (1987; 1993: 3–11) joins Iwamoto in disputing the authenticity of the *Yulanpen Sūtra*, adding a few more pieces of 'evidence' to the above list:

(5) There is no mention of filial devotion and submission or Mulian rescuing his mother (*Mulian jiumu*) in the *Sūtra Expounded by the Buddha on the Questions Raised by Maudgalyāyana Regarding the Five Hundred Light and Heavy Matters in the Vinaya* (*Fo shuo Mulian wen jielü zhong wubai qing zhong shi jing*), which, however, contains messages that are in direct contradiction to the conception of filial devotion such as the Buddhist *naiḥsargikapāyattika* (*sheduo*) injunctions against bhikṣus' purchasing shrouds and coffins for the burial of their deceased parents and against bhikṣus' supporting parents when they are still alive and are able to work to support themselves;
(6) There is no mention, either, of Mulian recusing his mother from Hell in the two famous Chinese Buddhist travel records, i.e. Monk Faxian's (ca. 337–422) *Record of Buddhist Kingdoms* (*Foguo ji*) and Monk Xuanzang's (602–664) *Great Tang Record of* [*Journeys to*] *the Western Regions* (*Da Tang xiyu ji*), nor is there any mention of this story in the *Biography of Sāriputra* or *Sāriputra-prakaraṇa* (*Shelifu zhuan*) – a Sanskrit drama by Aśvaghoṣa about Śāriputra and Maudgalyāyana converting to Buddhism;

(7) And there is no record of Mulian rescuing his mother in all the known Indic sources, where, however, there are references to Mulian's unfilial conduct towards his parents, as in the *Ekottarika āgama* and the *Mūlasarvāstivāda vinaya kṣudrakavastu*.

Zhu (1993: 8–11) goes further, claiming that:

(8) There was no such tradition in India as in China of making sacrificial offerings to one's deceased ancestors in the seventh lunar month; the Buddhist Yulanpen Festival on the fifteenth day of the seventh month was not based on the so-called *Yulanpen Sūtra* but instead modelled on the Daoist Middle-Primordial (Zhongyuan) Festival, which falls on the day of Middle-Primordial or the fifteenth day of the seventh month in Chinese lunar calendar – a holy day designated for offering sacrifices to 'the Officer of Earth Who Forgives Sins' (*diguan shizui*);

(9) And above all, filial piety and ancestor worship, which are native to Chinese culture and at the core of Confucianism, are in direct contradiction to Buddhism which advocates 'leaving home' (*chujia*) by severing family bonds and renouncing worldly ties to achieve enlightenment.

Hsiao (1995: 231–296; 1996: 83–98; 2005: 326–333), a highly productive Taiwanese scholar of Chinese religion and Chinese classics, expresses similar views to Zhu, although he seems to have been unaware of Zhu's publications made in mainland China on the sūtra, and he takes the argument even further than Iwamoto, Zhu and all the other above-named sceptics, asserting that:

(10) The *Yulanpen* Sūtra belittles Daoist priests (*daoshi*) by listing them among those who are powerless to rescue Mulian's mother from Hell, while magnifying the omnipotent power of the Saṃgha headed by the Buddha, thus betraying itself as an apocryphal scripture composed by Chinese Buddhists in response to or under the influence of the Daoist Zhongyuan Festival.

Refutation and Rebuttal

Upon close examination, however, hardly any of the above arguments hold water. Here below is a point-by-point refutation and rebuttal of them, beginning with the transmission and translation of Indian Buddhist texts.

Lost in transmission and regained in translation

The decades-long heated debate and discussion on the origin(s) of the *Yulanpen Sūtra* arises from the absence of the text in Indic sources known to us, which has been used by sceptics as the most direct evidence for their argument against the authenticity of the text. There is no denying the fact, but it does not necessarily follow from it that the sūtra is a Chinese Buddhist composition. This is because a considerable number of early Indian Buddhist texts were lost before taking the form of written artefacts, and to make matters worse, as Kornicki (2018: 217–218) notes, none of the original Buddhist manuscripts brought to China in the early period have survived, so no one can be absolutely certain whether the sūtra in the original ever existed in manuscript form and if so, whether it was among the lost Buddhist scriptures.

Indian Buddhist scriptures are half-buried literature. This is particularly true of Indic texts translated into Chinese in the first few centuries of the Common Era (Liang 1999: 13.3795–3797, 13.3837). The same may also be said of Buddhist texts brought to China at a later stage, given the fact that a great number of them translated by Monk Xuanzang (602–664), such as the *Yogācārabhūmi* (*Yujia shidi lun*) and *Mahāyānaśraddhotpāda śāstra* (*Dacheng qixin lun*), are not extant in Sanskrit or Tibetan translations (Delhey 2016: 52; Lung 2016: 103–104).

There are two major reasons for their failure to survive. The first one, as discussed in the previous chapter, is the early Buddhist oral tradition (oral origin, oral transmission and oral performance), which is highly reminiscent of the early (oral) stage of Gospel tradition (Dunn 2013); and the second is the virtual disappearance of Buddhism in the thirteenth century from the Indic heartland in the wake of the Islamisation of Central Asia and North Indian Plains.

Over one thousand years, more than one and a half thousand Buddhist texts were translated from Indian languages into Chinese, and many of them 'have not survived in their South Asian forms', as Barrett (2019) notes, but have persisted in the Chinese translations. It is therefore utterly preposterous to label these translations as apocryphal simply because their original Indic texts are not extant in the existing corpus of Indian Buddhist literature.

Dynamic equivalence in translation between the source text and the target text

Sceptics as represented by Iwamoto (1968, quoted in Zhu 1993: 8n; 1979: 9ff.) also single out Chinese words and expressions such as *wen ru shi*, *xiaoshun*, *liuqin* and *daoyan* found in the *Yulanpen Sūtra* as clear evidence for the spurious origin of the sūtra. These expressions are actually by no means 'bizarre expressions' as Iwamoto thinks. Rather, they make frequent appearances in pre-Kumārajīva (Jiumoluoshi, 334–413) translations. It is true that nearly all the post-Kumārajīva translations of sūtras begin with the tetra-syllabic formulaic expression of *ru shi wo wen* (Skr. *evaṃ mayā śrutam*), but it is far from being true of pre-Kumārajīva translations. And in fact, the omission of the first person pronoun in the shorter tri-syllabic phrase *wen ru shi* (Skr. *śrutam evaṃ*) is ubiquitous in virtually all the translations prior to the fifth century of Buddhist scriptures (Nattier 2014; see also Zürcher 1980 and Karashima 2013b: 289). This three-character formulaic expression was first employed by the pioneering translators An Shigao (fl. 148–180) and *Lokakṣema* (aka Zhi Loujiachen, fl. 147–189), subsequently adopted by their successors such as Zhi Qian (fl. ca. 223–252), Kang Senghui (d. 280) and Dharmarakṣa, and from then onwards became a standard opening for nearly all the translations of both Mahāyāna and non-Mahāyāna scriptures including Gāndhārī avadāna and pūrvayoga texts, up until the beginning of the fifth century when the four-character opening formula was introduced by Kumārajīva who added the first-person pronoun *wo* (Skr. *mayā*) to *wen ru shi*, hence the tetra-syllabic *ru shi wo wen*, and was immediately adopted by all major post-Kumārajīva translators. Indeed, the shift from the tri-syllabic phrase to the tetra-syllabic one is so profound that only twenty-four 'post-Kumārajīva' texts in the Taishō Canon are found still opening with the *wen ru shi* formula (Zürcher 1996: 2). Contrary to Iwamoto's claim, the fact that the *Yulanpen Sūtra* begins with *wen ru shi* instead of *ru shi wo wen* strongly suggests that this sūtra was a pre-Kumārajīva translation rather than a post-Kumārajīva creation.

As for the word *daoyuan* ('the eye of the Way') used in the *Yulanpen Sūtra* instead of *fayan* (Skr. *dharmacakṣus*) or *tianyan* (Skr. *divyacakṣus*) to refer to 'the divine eye' or 'clairvoyance' that Mulian acquires as part of his psychic power upon attaining arhathood, this Chinese word occurs nearly a hundred times in early Chinese translations from the Eastern Han period (AD 25–220) and also appears in Dharmarakṣa's translation of the *Saddharma puṇḍarīka sūtra* or *The Lotus Sūtra* (*Zheng fahua jing*, T09n0263_00 2.0073b20) as well. Compared with *daoyan*, the Chinese word *xiaoshun* enjoys an even higher frequency of occurrence in pre-Kumārajīva translations, where it appears more than 200 times, as noted by Karashima (2913b: 289n), although this word is often found in the translation of a Sanskrit word that does not carry the exact denotation or connotation of 'filial piety' as *xiaoshun* is understood in Chinese context. A good example of this is the (mis)use of *xiaoshun* in early Buddhist translations to render the Sanskrit term for Buddhist ethics *śīla*, meaning 'precept', 'virtue' or 'moral conduct' (Ma 1984: 19, quoted in Kumar 2005: 84–86).

Along the same line as Iwamoto, Xiong (2014: 89–90; 2015: 254–255) identifies *sangong* (lit. 'three ducal ministers') and *baiguan* (lit. 'hundred officials') in the *Yulanpen Sūtra* as evidence for this scripture being a Chinese Buddhist composition. Clearly, *sangong* and *baiguan* are used in the *Yulanpen Sūtra* to refer to 'court ministers' and 'officials of all ranks', respectively. There is no denying that these terms are unique to the bureaucratic system in ancient

China, but there is nothing incorrect or inappropriate about the use of an idiomatic, indigenous or culturally specific expression in the target (Sinitic) language to translate a conceptually relevant, similar or equivalent expression in the source (Indic) language – a strategy commonly employed by translators to achieve 'dynamic equivalence' between the source text and the target text.

'Dynamic equivalence' is a term coined by the American linguists and Biblical scholars Eugene Nida and Charles R. Taber (1969: 202) to refer to the 'quality of a translation in which the message of the original text has been so transported into the receptor language that the RESPONSE of the RECEPTOR is essentially like that of the original receptors'. The strategy for achieving dynamic equivalence in biblical translation finds an echo in the principle for sūtra translation postulated by the Eastern Jin Buddhist scholar and bibliographer Dao'an (314–385): '[Translators] must be faithful to the original while at the same time make sure their translation is intelligible to the general public' (*jixu qiuzhen youxue yusu*) (Quoted in Liang 1999: 13.3799). It thus comes as no surprise that 'When the Indian *nakṣatra*-s were first introduced to the Chinese through the Buddhist texts coming from Central Asia and India starting from the beginning of the first millennium CE', as Mak (2016: 145) observes, 'the translators naturally and conveniently matched them to their Chinese counterparts', a system of twenty-eight lunar asterisms known as *xiu* ('lodge' or 'mansion') developed during the Warring Sates period (476–221 BC) as recorded in the *Rites of Zhou* (*Zhouli* 26.180c, 37.251a, 40.276b) and *Master Lü's Annals of Spring and Autumn* (*Lüshi chunqiu* 13.1b-2a). Equally unsurprising is the use of Chinese lineage terms *liuqin* ('six types of relatives') and *qishi fumu* ('ancestors of past seven generations') to refer to one's family members, relatives and ancestors in the translation of the *Yulanpen Sūtra*.

Like *daoyan*, the Chinese word *daoshi* in the *Yulanpen Sūtra* has also been singled out as evidence for the spurious origin of this Buddhist scripture. Here, Hsiao (1995: 249–251; 2005: 328) goes even further than Iwamoto, claiming that the *Yulanpen Sūtra* exalts Buddhist monks and deprecates Daoist priests (*daoshi*) by listing *daoshi* among those who are powerless to rescue Mulian's mother from Hell as contrasted with the omnipotent Saṃgha headed by the Buddha. The context in which the word *daoshi* occurs in the scripture has (mis)led Hsiao to believe that the *Yulanpen Sūtra* was created as a Chinese Buddhist response to or under the influence of the Daoist Middle-Primordial Ceremony (*Zhongyuan fahui*). A close look at the text and the broader historical context where the word *daoshi* is used clearly demonstrates the fallacy in Hsiao's interpretation of *daoshi* as 'Daoist priest' and also in his use of this Chinese term as evidence to support his claim that the *Yulanpen Sūtra* was a Chinese Buddhist composition.

As revealed in the *Yulanpen Sūtra*, when Mulian came before the Buddha seeking his help and advice after he had tried in vain to feed the hungry ghost of his mother in Hell, the Buddha told him that it was all due to the grave sins his mother had committed when she was alive. The Buddha continued, saying to Mulian, 'Although your filial devotion and submission (*xiaoshun*) and your sound of crying have moved Heaven and Earth, there is nothing that heavenly gods, earthly deities, Māras, non-Buddhist monks (*waidao*), Buddhist monks (*daoshi*) and the Caturmahārājikādeva (Si tianwang shen) can do to save her'. Daoist priests or practitioners are, indeed, generally called in China *daoshi*, whereas Buddhist monks are commonly called *heshang*, *shamen* or *sengren*, the first deriving from the Sanskrit word *upādhyāya*, the second being a transliteration of the Sanskrit word *śramaṇa*[3] and the last a Chinese coinage from the Sanskrit, meaning a '*saṃgha* person'.

In the second and third centuries AD when Buddhist scriptures were first translated into Chinese, their translators found no equivalents in the Chinese language for many terms and expressions in the original Indic texts, so they borrowed terms and expressions from Chinese religious and philosophical texts, as observed by Monk Zongmi (780–841) in his explanatory notes on *waidao*, *daoshi* and Si tianwang shen in the *Yulanpen Sūtra* (*Yulanpen jing shu*, T39n1792_002.0510a09). Tang Yongtong (2006: 96, 103), a leading modern scholar of Chinese Buddhism, also notes that it was common practice to borrow 'Chinese native terms' (*Zhongtu mingci*) in early Chinese Buddhist translations, as shown in the translation of *muni* in the name of Buddha Śākyamuni ('the sage of the Śākya clan') into *nengren* (lit. 'be able to [practice] humanness') in the *Sūtra on the Rise of Buddhist Practice* or *Caryānidānasūtra* (*Xiuxing benqi jing*, T03n0184_001.0462b18), and in the interpretation of *muni* as *nengru* (lit. 'be able to [practice] Confucianism') in a side note provided by the third-century Chinese Buddhist translator, Zhi Qian (fl. ca. 223–252), in the *Sūtra on the Prince's Previous Incarnations with Auspicious Omens* or *Arthavargīyasūtra* (*Taizi ruiying benqi jing*, T03n0185_00 1.0473a15). The Chinese word *ren* (humanness; benevolence) is the most fundamental conception and virtue in Confucian ethics; as for *ru*, the term was originally used to designate 'masters of (funeral) rituals' or 'masters of techniques' in the Zhou dynasty (1045–256 BC), has been a general name for Confucianism and Confucian scholars since the Western Han dynasty (206 BC–AD 25).

The source from which Chinese native terms and expressions are borrowed in the translation of Buddhist scriptures is not limited to Confucianism. Chinese indigenous beliefs and religions – Daoism in particular – are also a major source of inspiration for translators of Buddhist scriptures. A case in point is *wuwei*,

3 The Sanskrit word *śramaṇa* is also often transliterated into *sangmen*, *suomen*, *shamenna*, *shaqiemennang*, *shimonanu*, *sheluomonu*, etc. in early Chinese Buddhist translations.

a key concept in Daoist philosophy meaning 'non-action' or 'taking no action', which is once used to render the Indic term, *nirvāṇa*, *nirvṛta* or *nirvṛti*, as noted by Deeg (2008: 111). Because there were no equivalents in Chinese to the Sanskrit words *upādhyāya* and *śramaṇa* and also because the transliteration of them respectively into *heshang* and *shamen* did not make much sense to Chinese people in the first place, the use of *dao*, *daoshi* and *waidao* to refer respectively to 'dharma', 'Buddhist monks' and 'non-Buddhist priests' became a convenient and expedient measure employed by pre-Kumārajīva translators of Buddhist scriptures. Buddhist monks continued, albeit less frequently than before, to be called *daoshi* in the Southern and Northern Dynasties (420–589) when Buddhism began to take roots in Chinese society. At the same time, they were also referred to as *daoren* (lit. 'Dao person'), and later they themselves coined the term *pindao*, meaning 'humble (follower of) Dao', as a self-referential form of address. Likewise, *daochang* (lit. 'Dao ground'), which is a Daoist term used to designate the sacred space for practicing Dao and also to refer to a well established Daoist ritual (Hiroshi 2008: 310–311), is also used to translate *bodhimaṇḍa*,[4] a Sanskrit word meaning 'seat of enlightenment' or 'platform of enlightenment', the place in BODHGAY under the BODHI TREE where the Buddha sat when he achieved liberation from the cycle of birth and death (SAṂS RA)' (Buswell and Lopez 2013: 317–318).

Clearly, the Chinese word *dao* in *daoyan*, *daoshi*, *daoren*, *daochang*, *pindao* and *waidao* as discussed above refers to the Buddhist Way rather than the Daoist or Confucian Way. It is thus fallacious to interpret *daoshi* as 'Daoist priests' in the *Yulanpen Sūtra* and even more so to conclude from the use of this term that the *Yulanpen Sūtra* is a Chinese Buddhist text composed to defame and calumniate Daoism.

The story of Mulian rescuing his mother: a recurring motif in ancient Indian literature

Another major argument presented by Iwamoto (1968, 1979) and Zhu (1987, 1993) against the authenticity of the *Yulanepn Sūtra* is that the story of Mulian rescuing his mother is not found elsewhere in sources from ancient India. While it is true that there is no extant the *Yulanpen Sūtra* in any known Indic

---

4 The earliest recorded use of *daochang* to translate *bodhimaṇḍa* appears in the *Sūtra Expounded by the Buddha on Infinite Purity, Impartiality and Enlightenment* or *Sukhūvatī vyūhasūtra* (*Foshuo wuliang qingjing pingdeng jue jing*, T12n0361_001. 0280b01), whose translation is conventionally attributed to *Lokakşema* (fl. AD 147-189), although modern and contemporary scholars such as Harrison (1998: 556–557), Nattier (2008: 86–87) and Karashima (2013a: 276–277) tend to credit Zhi Qian (fl. ca. 223–252) with translating this scripture. For more about the term *daochang* (*bodhimaṇḍa*) used in Chinese Buddhism, see Liu and Wang (2016: 189–228).

sources, it is far from being true that the content and theme of Mulian story is lacking in sources from ancient India. The *Manusmṛti* or *The Law of Manu*, for example, offers a brief account of a son called Puttra delivering his father from *put* or Hell (Bühler 2020). Another example is a story related in the Indian epic *Mahābhārata* about an ascetic rescuing his deceased ancestors from Hell (Ganguli 1883–1896: 13.55–56). The *Mahābhārata* story starts with the ascetic Jaratkaru seeing his ancestors hanging upside down in Hell due to his failure to marry and beget offspring and ends with Jaratkaru saving his ancestors from suffering by marrying and having children so that they may continue the family line and keep up offering of sacrifices to the ancestors. The Mulian story in the *Yulanpen Sūtra* is essentially the same as that in the non-Buddhist *Mahābhārata* and the *Manusmṛti* except that the protagonist in the Mulian story is a Buddhist monk who saves from Hell his mother instead of his father.

Actually, narratives about the Buddha and his chief disciples Śāriputra and Maudgalyāyana enlightening *preta* or hungry ghosts on the karmic retribution inflicted on them for the sins they had committed in their previous lives and also about hungry ghosts pleading with them to relieve their distress and rescue them from suffering in Hell abound in the Tripiṭaka, as exemplified in the *Scripture on the Karmic Retribution Against Hungry Ghosts* (*Egui baoying jing*, T17n0746), an anonymously translated text datable to the Eastern Jin (317–420) period, and also in the *Sūtra Expounded by the Buddha on Ghosts Questioning Maudgalyāyana* (*Fo shuo guiwen Mulian jing*, T17n0734), one of the first batches of Indian Buddhist texts translated into Chinese in the second century AD by the Parthian monk An Shigao (fl. 148–180).

We do not yet have direct evidence for the origin of the story in India of Mulian rescuing his mother, but we have ample indirect evidence that all points to the Mulian story related in the *Yulanpen Sūtra* being first and foremost an Indian one, although it contains elements of filial piety and ancestor worship that were highly valued in Confucian China. This kind of evidence abounds in the *Jātaka* (*Tales of Previous Lives of the Buddha*), and in particular, the *Avadānaśataka* (*Century of Noble Deeds*) and the *Petavatthu* (*Ghost Stories*). The *Avadānaśataka* is a Northern Buddhist collection of one hundred retribution cases or karma tales anonymously compiled in India with its first redaction datable to the second century AD at the earliest, whereas the *Petavatthu* is a Southern Buddhist work with its received text containing fifty-one ghost stories in verse form datable to the mid-fourth century at the earliest. The *Avadānaśataka* was translated into Chinese under the title of *Zhuanji baiyuan jing* (T04n0200, hereafter cited as *Baiyuan jing*) in ten sections or *vargas* (*pin*).[5] Most interesting to us is its fifth section titled 'Section on

5 The earliest known record of the *Avadānaśataka* in Chinese Buddhist bibliography appears in the *Catalogue of Collected Scriptures* (*Zhongjing mulu*, T55n2146_006.0144b08)

Hungry Ghosts' ('Egui pin'), which is devoted exclusively to accounts of the suffering and saving of hungry ghosts (*Baiyuan jing*, T04n0200_005.0222b18–0228a08). Although the *Avadānaśataka* and *Petavatthu* are from two different Buddhist traditions, many tales in them share the same theme, subject matter and rhetorical structure. A case in point is the recurring motif of 'rescuing the hungry ghost of a sinful mother', which also figures prominently in the Yulanpen story of Mulian rescuing his mother, as observed by Fujimoto (2003: 49) in his study of the origins of the *Yulanpen Sūtra*.

Included in the *Petavatthu*, for example, is a morality tale titled 'The Story of the Mother of the Elder Sāriputta', which is told by the Teacher, i.e. the Buddha, about Sāriputta making offerings to the Saṃgha and transferring the credit to the ghost of his sinful mother and thereby to rescue her from torture in the Peta realm (Gehman 1974: 2.*29–32*).[6] The story goes like this: One day Sāriputta, Moggallāna, Anuruddha, and Kappina are staying together in the forest near Rājagaha when a female hungry ghost (*peti*) approaches Sāriputta, saying that he was her son in her fifth life. Her husband, a wealthy Brahmin, was very generous and kind to beggars, tramps, wayfarers, monks and Brahmins all his life. He instructed her to provide food, drink, clothing and lodging for them while he was away from home. She consented but actually gave them nothing in his absence. Instead, she hurled insults at them and subjected them to various forms of humiliation. As a result, she was condemned to the Peta realm after death. The peti then asks Sāriputta to make offerings to the Saṃgha and to transfer the credit and merit to her. From King Bimbisara in Rājagaha, Sāriputta receives abundant gifts of food, drink and shelter. He presents them all to the Saṃgha headed by the Buddha and assigns to the peti the credit, thus successfully delivering the ghost of his mother from the Peta realm into the Deva realm. In this *Petavatthu* story, Moggallāna plays a minor yet essential role: he accompanies Sāriputta to Rājagaha seeking alms, reveals to the king the mother-son relationship between the peti and Sāriputta in their previous lives and eventually moves the king to give alms to the Sāriputta. Interestingly, the story ends with the peti, now a *deva* (celestial being), approaching Moggallāna and telling him in detail about both her peta and deva rebirths. The idea of karma and rebirth and the concept of merit accrual and transfer

---

compiled by Fajing and others, who credit the Indo-scythian upāsaka Zhi Qian (fl. ca. 223–252) as the translator. However, a close comparison of the Chinese and Sanskrit versions of *Avadānaśataka* and also that of the Chinese version with the mid-fifth century *Sūtra on the Wise and the Foolish* (*Xianyu jing*) lead Demoto Mitsuyo (1998: 26) to date the Chinese translation of *Avadānaśataka* to the late sixth century.

6 A Chinese version of this story is included in the *Scripture on Matters Related to Hungry Ghosts* (*Egui shi jing*, N28n0014_001.0015a05–0016a06).

demonstrated in this *Petavatthu* story are no different from those expounded by the Buddha through the Yulanpen story of Mulian making merit by offering up sacrifices to the Saṃgha, transferring the merit to the hungry ghost of his mother, rescuing her from Hell and eventually lifting her into Heaven.

'The Story of Uttara's Mother' is another prototypical example illustrating the motif of karmic retribution and reward (Gehman 1974: 2.54–56). This story features as the protagonist Uttara, a disciple of Śākyamuni Buddha known in Chinese as Youduoluo who is described in the *Collection of Texts Increasing by One* or *Ekottarika āgama* (*Zengyi ahan jing*, T02n0125_003.0557c03) as 'foremost [in meditation] among graves' (*zhongjian diyi*) for his habitual practice of meditation among graves. In this *Petavatthu* story, Uttara is portrayed as a devout layman who is very generous in providing clothing, bowl-food, medicine and dwelling for the venerable Mahākaccāyana and his disciples. In contrast, his mother is mean and vicious. Grudging his son's generous donations, she said, 'Whatever food and drink you give in this manner, without my consent, to recluses, may that become blood in your other world'. On one occasion, however, she donated a bunch of peacock tail-feathers to a Buddhist monastery. As a punishment for her blood curse, she died and was reborn as a peti suffering hunger and thirst. The moment she tried to drink from the Ganges, the river water would turn into blood. The peti had horrid appearance and timid look, but had black, glossy, curly, fine and long hair, which grew on her head as a reward for having donated the bunch of peacock tail-feathers to the monastery when alive. She revealed to the elder Kaṅkhārevata her deeds in the Manussa realm and her sufferings in the Peta realm. In her name, the venerable monk gave alms (water, food and bark-clothes) to the Saṅgha, thereby delivering the peti out of the Peta realm into the Deva realm. Worthy of notice is that her blood curse on Uttara was later turned back against herself after her death because the water would turn into blood before she could drink it, which is highly reminiscent of the horror scene of the cooked rice turning into burning charcoal before entering the mouth of Mulian's mother in the *Yulanpen Sūtra*.

Uttara and his sinful mother are also featured in the 'Causal Condition of Uttara's Mother Falling into the Peta Realm' ('Youduoluo mu zhui egui yuan') in the *Avadānaśataka* (*Baiyuan jing*, T04n0200_005.0224c17–0225b23).[7] This *Avadānaśataka* story is set in Rājagaha, where lived an elder of great wealth and resources. He took a high-born woman to wife, entertaining her with music and performance every day. Ten months later, his wife gave birth

7 A shorter and slightly different version of this story is included in the *Differentiated Manifestations of the Sūtra and Vinaya Piṭaka* (*Jinglü yixiang*, T53n2121_019.0107b03), where a Buddhist text titled *Scripture of Uttara's Mother* (*Youduoluo mu jing*) is given as the Indic source of this story.

to a beautiful baby boy, whom they named Uttara with great pride. When Uttara grew up, his father died but the young man refused to inherit and continue his family business. Instead, he asked his mother for permission to leave home and become a monk. His mother rejected his request, saying that she would rather die than let him leave home. Uttara was very upset and threatened to take his own life if she refused. To comfort his son, the woman promised to provide food and accommodation for itinerant śramaṇas and Brahmins, but she soon regretted having made the promise. Every time when Uttara was away from home, she would abuse and insult śramaṇas and Brahmins who lodged in her house as arranged by his son. She even threw food and drink onto the ground rather than give them to eat. But every time when his son returned, she would treat them very well as if they were her distinguished guests, which made Uttara very happy. Surely as expected, she died and sank into the Preta realm. After her death, Uttara left home to become a monk and quickly achieved arhathood. One day, Uttara was sitting in meditation on a riverbank when a preta approached him, saying that she was his mother. Uttara did not believe the preta, thinking to himself that her mother could not have been reborn as a preta because she had been very generous and kind to monks and recluses when alive. The preta then confessed to Uttara that she had deceived him and had thus been condemned to the Preta realm, where she had been given nothing to eat or drink ever since her death twenty years ago. She asked Uttara to give alms to recluses to atone for her sins so that she would be rescued from Naraka or Hell. Uttara performed a sacrificial ritual of making offerings to monks at the request of the preta of his sinful mother. She appeared at the ceremony to make public confession and atonement for her sins. Eventually, the World-Honoured One rescued the preta from Naraka and lifted her into the Trāyastriṃśa (*daolitian*) or Heaven of the Thirty-Three. This is a story about a family of three as in the *Yulanpen* story of Mulian – father, mother and son: Uttara is a pious youth, father a wealthy yet devout man, whereas mother a stingy and deceptive woman.

Indeed, retribution, reward, rescue and rebirth are themes and motifs that interweave and recur throughout Mahāyāna and Theravāda Buddhist scriptures, and many of them, as exemplified by the Mulian story in the *Yulanpen Sūtra*, the Sāriputta story and the Uttara story in the *Petavatthu* and the Uttara story in the *Avadānaśataka*, involve a devout and filial son rescuing the hungry ghost of his sinful mother from Hell. Although each of the hungry ghost stories discussed above features a different disciple of the Buddha, they bear striking resemblance to one another in characterisation, setting, structure, storyline and subject matter. They are identical to one another in so many respects and details that they read very much like three different versions of one and the same story of a monk recusing the ghost of his sinful mother from Hell and bringing her rebirth in Heaven by making offerings on her behalf to the Buddha and the Saṃgha and transferring the merits to the ghost. It is therefore groundless to claim that the content of the Mulian story is not found elsewhere in sources from ancient India except in the 'apocryphal' *Yulanpen Sūtra*.

As mentioned above, Iwamoto (1968) notes the 'absence' in Indian Buddhist literature of the content of the Mulian story and uses it as evidence to prove that the *Yulanpen Sūtra* does not originate from India. While holding the same view as Iwamoto (1968; 1979) and Zhu (1987; 1993) that the *Yulanpen Sūtra* is a Chinese Buddhist apocryphal scripture, Hsiao (2005: 328–331) admits the existence in the so-called authentic Buddhist scriptures of the recurring motif of a filial son or a devout monk rescuing the ghost of his sinful mother but ironically uses it as evidence to justify his suspicion that Dharmarakṣa forged the *Yulanpen Sūtra* by transplanting the *Avadānaśataka* story of Uttara into the *Yulanpen* story of Mulian.

Mulian in Sanskrit and Tocharian drama

Zhu (1993: 3–11, esp. 8n) owes much of his inspiration to Iwamoto (1968; 1979) in disputing the authenticity of the *Yulanpen Sūtra*. He (1993: 4–5) checks through the *Record of Buddhist Kingdoms* (*Foguo ji*) and the *Great Tang Record of [Journeys to] the Western Regions* (*Da Tang xiyu ji*, T51n2087; hereafter cited as *Xiyu ji*), finding in them no record whatsoever of Mulian travelling to Hell to rescue his mother, and produces it as further evidence that the sūtra alongside the Mulian story is a Chinese Buddhist composition.

Also known as the *Biography of the Eminent Monk Faxian* (*Gaoseng Faxian zhuan*, T51n2085; hereafter cited as *Faxian zhuan*), the *Record of Buddhist Kingdoms* is a journal written by Faxian (ca. 337–422) of his pilgrimage through Central Asia to India and Ceylon in search of Buddhist scriptures; and the *Great Tang Record of [Journeys to] the Western Regions* was compiled by Bianji (619–649), one of Xuanzang's (602–634) most trusted assistants and disciples, on the basis of Xuanzang's own records of his travel to Central Asia and India. From their failure to mention the Mulian story and the *Yulanpen Sūtra* in their travel records, Zhu (1993: 5) infers that there has never existed such story or sūtra in India about Mulian rescuing his mother from Hell. This inference is problematic, for it is neither necessary nor possible for travellers to note down all they saw or heard. It would be as absurd to hereby conclude that the Mulian story along with the *Yulanpen Sūtra* is a Chinese Buddhist creation as to conclude that the *Precepts on Miscellaneous Matters of the Mūlasarvāstivāda School* or *Mūlasarvāstivāda vinaya kṣudrakavastu* (*Genbenshuo yiqieyou bu pinaiye zashi*, T24n1451_018) is a Chinese Buddhist apocryphal scripture simply because the karm story of Mulian meeting a violent death recounted in this Vinaya text is not mentioned in either of the two travel records from medieval China.

In a similar vein, Zhu (1993: 7–8) makes a special mention of the *Biography of Śāriputra* or *Śāriiputra prakaraṇa* (*Shelifu zhuan*) in his assertion that the *Yulanpen Sūtra* is a Chinese Buddhist apocryphal scripture. The *Śāriputra prakaraṇa*, the oldest Sanskrit drama known to us, fails to survive in its entirety. Fragments of it, dating from the fourth century AD, were discovered during the German Expeditions (1902–1914) to Turfan in Xinjiang (BBASH 2007: 6). The German Indologist Heinrich Lüders (1911) successfully reconstructed from the fragments the *Śāriputra prakaraṇa* – a dramatic text in nine acts – and identified the great Sanskrit poet and Buddhist scholar Aśvaghoṣa as its author. In his comparative study of Sanskrit drama and Chinese drama, Xu Dishan (1927: 32) notes that there is no such story as that of Mulian saving his mother included or mentioned in the *Biography of Śāriputra*, which is cited by Zhu (1993: 7n) as further evidence for the non-existence of the Mulian story or the *Yulanpen Sūtra* in Indic sources. From Lüders' reconstructed text, however, we know that the *Sāriputra prakaraṇa* is centred on the conversion of Śāriputra and Maudgalyāyana by the Buddha. With focus on Buddhist conversion rather than Buddhist salvation, it is perfectly understandable that the drama makes no mention of Śāriputra or Maudgalyāyana feeding and saving the hungry ghost of their mothers. Actually, the mere absence of the Mulian story in the drama cannot prove either the existence or non-existence of the Mulian story in Indic sources, just as the lack of convincing evidence for the existence of alien beings in the world of human beings cannot prove or disapprove the existence of alien beings in other realms of existence unknown to us. The problem with Zhu's argument here, as with that of many other sceptics, is that absence of evidence is confused with evidence of absence.

It is worth mentioning, however, that among the fragmentary texts collected by the German Expeditions to Turfan is an incomplete text of *Maitreyasamiti Nāṭaka* or *Drama on Encounter with Maitreya*, which was written in Tocharian A, an extinct Indo-European language once spoken in the Turfan region (BBASH 2007: 11).[8] In April 1959, fragments of a dramatic text that has come to be known as *Maitrisimit nom bitig* or *Meeting with Maitreya* (*Mile huijian ji*) was discovered by a shepherd in Hami of Xinjiang (Wu 1960; Feng 1962) and was edited by Israpil Yüsüp et al. (1988) into *Qădimqi Uighur Yezighidiki Maitrı Simit* (*Huihuwen Mile huijian ji*). Copied by hand on 293 leaves, the *Maitrisimit nom*

8 Having deciphered the Tocharian language in the fragmentary text, Emil Sieg and Wilhelm Siegling (1921) published the text in two volumes with Volume One containing facsimiles and Volume Two the romanised transliteration of the text.

Figure 4.1 Fragments of *Maitrisimit nom bitig*. Size: 22 cm × 44 cm.

Source: Xinjiang Uyghur Autonomous Region Museum. Photo by the author.

bitig is an Old Uighur/Turkic version of the *Maitreyasamiti Nāṭaka* (Figure 4.1). The Tocharian A version and the old Uighur version of the drama are datable to the eighth and ninth century, respectively (Ji 2011: 3).

In March 1975, forty-four leaves of the manuscript remains of a Tocharian A version of the drama were discovered at the site of a Tang dynasty (618–907) Buddhist monastery called 'Qige xing' ('Seven Stars') in Yanqi, Xinjiang and identified as another handwritten copy of the drama (Ji 2011). Interestingly, this drama contains a rescue story concerning Maudgalyāyana and his mother. Out of admiration for 'the holy of the holiest virtue' of Mahāmaudgalyāyana the noble Arhat, Mariqi the Queen of Heaven travels tens and thousands of miles and climbs over one after another peak of Mount Meru to see the Buddha of Heaven with a request for him to save Maudgalyāyana's mother; the Buddha descends to the world, appears in the Kingdom of Ghadegadha and saves Maudgalyāyana's mother on account of his 'holy of the holiest virtue' (*Qădimqi Uighur Yezighidiki Maitri Simit*, leaf 5, lines 11–13a).

As stated in the colophon to the Hami text (quoted in Adams 1988: 2–3):

> The sacred book *Maitreya-samiti* which the Bodhisattva guru ācārya Āryacandra, who was born in the country of Nagaradeśa [*sic*], had composed in the Twγry languages out of the Indian language, and which the guru ācārya Prajñarakṣita, who was born in Il-bliq, translated from the Twγry language into the Turkish language.

Thus, we know that the *Maitrisimit nom bitig* had been composed in Twγry (*toxrï*, commonly known as Tocharian A) by a certain Āryacandra (Shengyue, literally maning 'the holy moon'), who was born in Qārāšahr (Uig. Karasahr; Ch. Yanqi) in present-day Xinjiang, on the basis of the Indic *Maitreyasamiti Nātaka*, before being translated by Prajñarakṣita into Old Turkic/Uighur. We may also infer from the colophon that the *Maitreyasamiti Nāṭak* contains one brief reference to Śākyamuni the Buddha of Heaven saving Maudgalyāyana's mother at the request of Mariqi the Queen of Heaven as found in its Old Turkic/Uighur version, i.e. *the Maitrisimit nom bitig.* A further inference may also be made that both Mariqi and Śākyamuni rush to her rescue because of the holy virtue of Maudgalyāyana. It is not clear, however, as to exactly what kind of holy virtue(s) Maudgalyāyana has that moves Mariqi and Śākyamuni to rescue his mother, what trouble or danger she is in and needs to be delivered from, let alone what causal condition of her trouble or danger is. There seems to be no end to a list of questions like this because of the fragmentary and marginal nature of this short episode in the overall narrative and thematic structure of the *Maitrisimit nom bitig.* In any case, however, this dramatic episode in the *Maitrisimit nom bitig* echoes the motif presented in the *Yulanpen Sūtra* of retribution, reward and rescue that recurs throughout Indian Buddhist literature.

Mulian and the Buddha as negative examples for the law of karma

One other major reason that Zhu (1993: 5–6) denies the authenticity of the *Yulanpen Sūtra* is that Maudgalyāyana is never portrayed – except in the 'apocryphal' *Yulanpen Sūtra* – as a pious son but instead as an unfilial son in Indian Buddhist scriptures, giving the *Precepts on Miscellaneous Matters of the Mūlasarvāstivāda School* (*Mūlasarvāstivāda vinaya kṣudrakavastu*) as an example to illustrate his point. This Vinaya scripture does record a story told by the Buddha about a past life of Maudgalyāyana in which he was born as a human son into a Brahmin family (*Genbenshuo yiqieyou bu pinaiye zashi*, T24n1451_018.0290b05). When Maudgalyāyana grew up and got married, he developed a grudge against his parents for their disapproving of him spoiling his wife, and he even 'intended to get a strong man to smash his parents into pieces like squashed reeds' (Ibid.). As a matter of fact, this is a story embedded in a larger story of paying karmic debt in which Maudgalyāyana ends up crushed, smashed and torn into pieces by non-Buddhist heretics in retribution merely for the evil intention he had once conceived against his parents in a previous life of his.

A similar story titled 'Death of Moggallāna the Great' appears in the *Commentary to the Dhammapada* or *Dhammapadaṭṭhakathā* (Burlingame 2020), a text comprised of stories similar to those in the *Jātaka* and conventionally ascribed to Buddhaghosa (fl. fifth century). This story starts with a group of non-Buddhists bribing local rascals and robbers to beat Moggallāna and tear his body into pieces out of their hatred for Moggallāna having successfully persuaded people into giving all their donations to the Buddha and his followers. Before breathing his last, Moggallāna 'felt the compelling force of the evil deed he had himself committed in a previous state of existence, and made no attempt to get away', although he could have easily escaped from the ambush or subdued his attackers if he had exercised his psychic power. The local monastic community of Buddhism was plunged into fear and confusion as to why 'Elder Moggallāna the Great had met a death that he did not deserve'. Then the Buddha approached them, revealing to them that the tragic death of Moggallāna had come along as the karma of having committed the grave crime of parenticide in a past life of his by luring his blind parents into a forest and murdering them in order to please his wife who had grudged against her parents-in-law for their envy of their son's love for her. These two Avadāna stories each deal with one of the numerous previous lives that Moggallāna had lived before attaining arhathood and achieving nirvāṇa. Obviously, they are meant to expound the inescapability and invincibility of karmic retribution. It is therefore ridiculous to cite the Avadāna stories about the former incarnations of Moggallāna as evidence to disprove the authenticity of *Yulanpen Sūtra* as a Buddhist scripture translated from some Indic source(s).

Actually, even the Buddha himself was not free of past bad karma, nor was he exempt from karmic retribution for the bad karma built up in his previous lives, although Gotama Siddhārtha is recorded having lived a life endowed with physical and spiritual perfection in the Buddha biography preserved in the Pāli Tipiṭaka, particularly the Vinaya Piṭaka and the Sutta Piṭaka and having produced an enormous amount of good karma recorded in the Jātaka/Avadāna tales (Walters 1990). Accounts of less pleasant events in his life are found in the canon of both Mahāyāna and Theravāda Buddhism. The *Long Discourses* or *Dīrghāgama* (*Chang ahan jing*, T01n001_002.0015b16), for example, records such an event in which the Buddha suffered from acute backache about three months before he entered into nirvāṇa at the age of eighty. It turns out that the Buddha's backache arose from his previous bad karma as noted in the 'Sūtra Expounded by the Buddha on the Backache-giving Karma' ('Fo shuo beitong suyuan jing'), a Jātaka/Avadāna story included in the *Sūtra Expounded by the Buddha on Causes and Conditions* (*Foshuo xingqi xing jing*, T04n0197_001.0167c02–0167c26), which is a collection of ten Avadāna tales told by the Buddha about bad karma from his many past lives.[9] This story presents *the* Buddha as a strong man in a past life of his.

9 This sūtra is listed by Monk Sengyou (445–518) in the 'Catalogue of a New Collection of Subsequently Composed, Anonymously Translated Miscellaneous Scriptures' ('Xinji xuzhuan shiyi zajing lu') of his *Compilation of Notices on the Translation of the Tripiṭaka* (*Sanzang jiji* T55n2145_004.0021b18), and for this reason, among others,

He was engaged in a wrestling match during a festival with another strong man, a former incarnation of Devadatta. Devadatta was a brother of Ānanda and a cousin of the Buddha, who is described in Pāli Tipiṭaka as the greatest enemy of the Buddha that attempted to murder the Buddha (Penner 2009). Before the match kicked off, Devadatta promised to let the Buddha have the reward from the king if the Buddha let him win, but because Devadatta had cheated the Buddha of the championship and reward by making the same promise many times before, the Buddha decided not to allow himself to be fooled again, so he held Devadatta by the neck, brought his arm down on his back, threw him onto the ground and killed him, thus winning the match and being rewarded by the king with 100,000 coins. At the end of the story, the Buddha told Śāriputra, 'Greed and anger arose in me, causing me to kill Devadatta. I was therefore condemned to Hell and suffered there for thousands of years. Now that I have become enlightened and have eliminated all afflictions, I am still suffering from backache, which is the bad karma from those actions'.

Clearly, the Buddha told Śāriputra this story with a view to enlightening him as to the origin of suffering being the cause of suffering, greed, anger and killing being the cause of bad karma and bad karma being the cause of endless reincarnation. The cause, condition and consequence of bad karma from the former incarnations of the Buddha find their full expression in the so-called 'nine karmic paybacks' (*jiu zui bao*) in the *Great Treatise on the Perfection of Wisdom* or *Mahāprajñāpāramitāsāstra* (*Da zhidu lun*, T25n1509_009). The Buddha used his former incarnation as a negative example to urge his followers to guard their mental, verbal and physical action and to refrain from creating bad karma in this life, and for the same purpose, the Buddha told the Avadāna stories about Maudgalyāyana being an unfilial son and committing parenticide in one of his previous lives. Thus, it would be equally ridiculous to reject these scriptures as apocryphal simply because they promote the Buddhist law of karma by negative examples about the Buddha and his disciples.

Buddha on filial piety and ancestor worship

To back up his claims, Zhu (1993: 4) produces as further evidence that the *Sūtra Expounded by the Buddha on the Questions Raised by Maudgalyāyana Regarding*

Nattier (2008: 102–109, 177) excludes this scripture from the translations by Kang Mengxiang (fl. AD 194), although Kang is usually credited as its translator in later Chinese catalogues of Buddhist canon.

the Five Hundred Light and Heavy Matters in the Vinaya (*Fo shuo Mulian wen jielü zhong wubai qing zhong shi jing*, T24n1483b; hereafter cited as *Mulian wen jielü*) makes no mention of filial piety or Maudgalyāyana travelling to Hell to rescue his mother. Instead, the sūtra (*Mulian wen jielü*, T24n1483b_001.0989c21), he (1993: 4) notes, contains Buddhist injunctions that are apparently contradictory to the ethical value of filial piety promoted in the *Yulanpen Sūtra* by prohibiting bhikṣus from purchasing shrouds and coffins to bury their deceased parents and from supporting their parents when they are still alive and able to work to support themselves.

At this point, Zhu demonstrates complete disregard for evidence unfavourable to him. In actual fact, the Buddha keeps reminding his disciples of the importance of parental respect in his dialogue with Mulian and even urges them to show as much respect for their parents as for the Buddha's image and Buddhist precepts. For example, when asked about what offence a bhikṣu commits if he sells the Buddha's image, the Budda replies, 'Thus, he commits an offence publishable as for selling his parents' (*Mulian wen jielü*, T24n1483b_001.0985a29); and when asked about the offence of burning Buddhist precepts, the Buddha answers, 'If he does not know it is an offence to burn them, his act is a misdemeanour (Ch. *sheduo*; Skr. *naiḥsargikapāyattika*), but if he knows it is an offence, his act is publishable as for burning his parents' (*Mulian wen jielü*, T24n1483b_001.0985b29).

In this Vinaya scripture, the Buddha does discourage his disciples from supporting their parents when they are still able to work to support themselves, but at the same time, the Buddha makes it absolutely clear that if their parents are ill and unable to support themselves, they should let their parents half of the food they have begged (*Mulian wen jielü*, T24n1483b_001.0989c21). When asked about whether it is or not in conformity with the [Buddhist] principle for bhikṣus to instruct laypeople (*baiyi*) to make no sacrificial offerings to deceased persons whoever they are, the Buddha says, 'Not at all. Even if one's [deceased] parents do not partake of the food offerings, one will still be able to receive blessings from one's parents in return for one's making offerings with filial devotion (*jingxin gongyang*) (*Mulian wen jielü*, T24n1483b_002.0993b11). Obviously, the Buddha not only instructs his disciples to respect their parents and support them when they are in need but also exhorts people to make offerings to the dead including their deceased parents and ancestors because they will be blessed for their sacrificial offerings.

Here, the Buddha shows no objection to ancestor worship, let alone filial piety. On the contrary, the Buddha demonstrates himself as a filial son, always ready to repay the kindness of his mother for bearing him even after attaining Buddhahood, as shown in the *Sūtra of Queen Maya* or

Mahāmāyāsūtra (*Mohemoye jing*, T12n0383).[10] After entering nirvāṇa, as we are told, the Buddha miraculously ascended the Trāyastriṃśa and spent the three months of the rainy-season retreat (*vārsika*) there preaching the Dharma to his mother Mahāmāyā, who died seven days after giving birth to the future buddha and was reborn in the Tuṣita Heaven (*doushuaitian*). The Buddha awakened her to her karma (*suming*) and roots of good (*shangen*) or *kuśalamūla* and delivered her from the karmic cycle of suffering through rebirths and redeaths (*Mohemoye jing*, T12n0383_001.1005c08). In so doing, the Buddha 'repays the kindness of his mother for bearing him and demonstrates his filial love (*xiaolian*) for her', thereby setting a good example for 'all unfilial sentient beings' (*buxiao zhu zhongsheng*) to follow (*Mohemoye jing*, T12n0383_002. 1013a07–1013a25).

Filial piety and ancestor worship as a living tradition in the Indic world

Among the various reasons and types of evidence provided by the sceptics against the authenticity of the *Yulanpen Sūtra*, the most common and compelling is the theme of filial piety that underlies the sūtra in close association with that of ancestor worship. In their view (e.g. Ch'en 1964: 179; 1968: 81–82), filial piety and ancestor worship are central to Confucianism but are somewhat peripheral, if not entirely alien, to Indian culture, and flatly contradict the Buddhist pursuit of *nirvāṇa* by severing family bonds and renouncing worldly ties to achieve enlightenment in dharma. Thus, they regard the *Yulanpen Sūtra* as part of the effort made by Chinese Buddhists to adapt Indian Buddhism to Confucian filial ethics and to make it acceptable to Chinese people.

Ch'en (1968: 82–83; 1973: 18) notes that there are in general three ways of Buddhism adapting to Chinese filial ethics:

> [F]irst, by pointing out the numerous sutras in the Buddhist canon which stress filial piety; second, by forging a body of apocryphal literature which emphasizes piety as its central theme; and third, by

---

10 Translated by Monk Tanjing (fl. 479-502), the *Mohemoye jing* is alternatively titled *Fo sheng daolitian weimu shuofa* (*The Buddha Ascends the Trāyastriṃśa Heaven to Preach the Dharma to His Mother*), which is related to but different from the *Sūtra of the Buddha's Ascension to the Trāyastriṃśa Heaven to Preach the Dharma to His Mother* (*Fo sheng daolitian weimu shoufa jing*, T17n0815), a fourth-century text attributed to Dharmarakṣa (d. 308) as the translator, which features Maudgalyāyana rather than Mahāmāyā as an interlocutor with the Buddha, albeit otherwise suggested by its title.

> contending that the Buddhist concept of filial piety was superior to that of Confucians in that it aimed at universal salvation (this would include all previous ancestors in different forms), while the Confucian piety was limited to just one family.

Clearly, filial piety and ancestor worship are viewed by the sceptics as the most prominent features that distinguish Chinese Buddhist scriptures from Indian Buddhist scriptures and therefore as the most direct and decisive evidence for their claims and arguments.

Indeed, filial piety was emphasised in China long before the spread of Buddhism from India to China around the first century AD, and so was ancestor worship, but filial piety and ancestor worship are by no means alien to Indian culture. Instead, they were also an important and integral part of social and religious life in ancient India (Strong 1983; Schopen 1984; Xing 2016). Scriptural and archaeological evidence for the importance of filial piety and ancestor worship in the development and practice of Buddhism in India abounds. There are extant hundreds of inscriptions – mostly from early Buddhist Ceylon and Northwest India – about the ritual of *pūjā* performed to make offerings for the wellbeing of one's living and deceased parents. As recorded in these inscriptions, the donors performed their act of 'offering' in the belief that they could transfer it to their parents, ancestors and descendants (Schopen 1984: 116; see also Tillakaratne 1986: 169f.), and significantly, more than half of the donors were monks and nuns, including senior members of the Buddhism community (Schopen 1984: 119, 122–123). It is clear from these inscriptions that Buddhist belief and practice had come under the influence of Indian filial ethics well before they spread to China.

In an in-depth study of Buddhist rituals of death and rebirth in contemporary Sri Lanka and their Indian origins, Langer (2007: 148–163, esp. 158–160) notes that offering food (*śrāddha*) whereby merit is transferred to ancestors is deeply rooted in pre-Buddhist Vedic traditions and has been incorporated into Buddhist post-funeral rites that are widely observed in contemporary Sri Lanka. At the core of the ritual, Langer (2007: 152–153, 159, 188) argues, are ancestor worship and filial piety that are still held in high regard in India and Sri Lanka.

A remarkable feature of Indian filial ethics, however, is its emphasis on the bond between mother and son and on son's devotion to his mother (Lardinois 1996: 595; Cole 1998: 2; Hinsch 2002: 51, 53). This is somewhat different to the Confucian moral teachings on filial piety, which revolves around the relationship between father and son with particular emphasis on the obedience of son to father. When asked what is meant by *xiao* (filial piety), Confucius (551–479 BC) is quoted in the *Analects* (*Lunyu* 1.2b) as saying:

> When his father is alive, observe his intentions. After his father is dead, observe his actions. If for three years there is no change [he makes] to his father's way, he may be considered filial.

Confucian emphasis on filial devotion and submission to one's father recorded in the *Analects* is reaffirmed in a dialogue between Confucius and his disciple Zengzi (505–435 BC) quoted in the Confucian *Classic of Filial Piety* (*Xiaojing* 5.15a):

> Zengzi asked, 'May I venture to ask whether there is anything in the virtue of the sages that is greater than filial piety?' The Master replied, 'In the nature of Heaven and Earth, the human is the noblest; in human behaviour, nothing is greater than filial piety; in filial piety, nothing is greater than the reverential awe of one's father.'

When Buddhism was introduced to China, it was inevitably brought into direct contact and conflict with indigenous Chinese ideas, values and beliefs represented by Confucianism. The overall relationship between Buddhism and Confucianism was a dynamic, bidirectional process though. A case in point is the translation and transformation of *xiao*. As discussed above, the Chinese culture-specific term *xiao/xiaoshun* was used in the translation of Buddhist scriptures like the *Yulanpen Sūtra* in order for them to be accessible and acceptable to Chinese people. However, Buddhism did not merely borrow or assimilate Confucian principles of filial piety. Buddhism also influenced and even transformed Confucian practices of filial piety, as exemplified by the shift of the focus of filial devotion from father to mother in medieval and early modern China (Cole 1998). In this dynamic process, the *Yulanpen Sūtra* plays an important role due to its great influence and popularity among both the general public and the ruling and educated elite and also due to its seamless integration of filial piety with ancestor worship in the dharma.

Confucian filial ethics not only emphasises one's dedication and obedience to one's parents when they are alive but also stresses the importance of performing memorial services and offering sacrifices to one's deceased ancestors. The Master instructed his disciples to 'sacrifice to [their ancestors] as if they were present and to sacrifice to [their] spirits as if they were present' (*Lunyu* 3.11a). Likewise, the Indian version of filial piety also takes a two-fold practical form of a) dedicating oneself to one's parents and b) offering sacrifice to one's parents and ancestors, as convincingly demonstrated by Schopen (1984) through his study of the epigraphical material from ancient India and Ceylon. Not coincidently, the Chinese word *ru*, as the generic appellation for 'Confucianism' and

'Confucian scholars', was originally applied to specialists in rituals, particularly funeral rituals in pre-Confucian times (*Mozi* 9.291; see also Hu 1986).

As in Confucianism and Daoism, filial piety is interconnected with ancestor worship in Buddhism and Hinduism, which is fully manifested in the ritual of *śrāddha* dedicated to one's deceased fathers and ancestors (*pitṛs*). With its roots in the ancient Vedic sacrificial culture, the śrāddha rite is a living tradition that is still performed in contemporary India as funeral offerings made to one's deceased parents (Langer 2007: 152) as well as in Theravāda countries in Southeast Asia (Figure 4.2). At the heart of the ritual is the belief in the transference of merit to one's deceased ancestors and the transposition of them from the Pretaloka to the Devaloka or the Pitṛloka – the heavenly realm of the ancestors who live on the food offered to them – through the ritual offerings and the offering rituals (Sayers 2013: 2).

The śrāddha rite is both a social and religious ceremony performed by male descendants for both their deceased parents and ancestors on both paternal and maternal sides. Brief accounts of and references to the ritual of śrāddha are numerous in Buddhist literature, particularly in the Nikāyas and Āgamas in the Pāli Tipiṭaka (Sayers 2013: 86–99; Xing 2016). Top on the list of the few primary offerings to ancestors are rice balls as recorded in the *Gṛhyasūtras* or *Sūtras on Domestic Rites* (Sayers 2013: 64), which is highly

Figure 4.2 People make merits to commemorate the traditional Tenth Lunar Month Festival or Sat Thai Day (Śrāddha Festival), Surat Thani Province, Thailand, 21 September 2017. Photo courtesy of Phra Kiattisak Kittipanyo.

reminiscent of the dramatic scene depicted in the *Yulanpen Sūtra* of Mulian filling a bowl with cooked rice and feeding the hungry ghost of his mother. Considering the central importance of rice balls as sacrificial offerings designated for domestic ancestral rites in the Vedic ritual texts, it seems not unlikely at all that *yulan* is a transliteration of a Middle Indic form **olana* ('boiled rice'), as suggested by Karashima (2013b).

Historical links between Lafo/Yulanpen and Pavāraṇā/Kaṭhina

The origin of the *Yulanpen* Festival is a most central and controversial issue that underlies the debate and discussions on the authenticity of the *Yulanpen Sūtra*. Although, as Zhu (1993: 7–8) points out, no mention is made of the Mulian story in the Chinese Buddhist travel records, they all contain valuable information that is of great help to us in tracing the ritual roots of the Yulanpen Festival in Buddhist India.

At the end of the *Record of Buddhist Kingdoms*, for example, Monk Faxian offers a vivid account of his homeward voyage from Ceylon via Java. Thus, we know that in 412 or the eighth year of Yixi (405–419) of the Eastern Jin dynasty, Monk Faxian and his fellow passengers reached the shore on the south of Mount Lao or Laoshan in Changguang, Qingzhou prefecture (now part of Qingdao, Shandong province). After landing ashore, they met two hunters, who claimed to be the Buddha's followers, saying that they 'are picking peaches as offerings to be presented to the Buddha (*lafo*)' because 'tomorrow is the fifteenth day of the seventh month' (*Faxian zhuan*, T51n2085_001.0865c24). They were lying, Faxian notes, when they claimed to be followers of the Buddha because they thought Faxian who himself was a Buddhist monk would be delighted to be told so, but they immediately realised that the Buddha's followers would not go hunting to take life, so they added that they were picking peaches for the upcoming Lafo Ceremony. The first statement is an honest-to-goodness lie and the second a half-truth with respect to the ritual of sacrifice to the Buddha on the fifteenth day of the seventh month. Thus, it is very likely that by the early fifth century at the latest, the fifteenth day of the seventh month had been designated for the Buddhist Lafo Ceremony, which came to be celebrated in the sixth century as the Yulanpen Ceremony.

Closely related to the Lafo Ceremony of making offerings to the Buddha on the fifteenth day of the seventh month is the 'rainy-season (summer) retreat' (Skr. *vārsika/varṣa*; Pāli: vassa), which is variously referred to as *zuoxia*, *xiazuo*, *anju* and *xia anju* in the *Record of Buddhist Kingdoms*. The *Mahāsāṃghika vinaya* or *Monastic Rules of the Great Saṃgha School* (*Mohe sengqi lü*, T22n1425), one of the three Vinaya texts brought back to China from Central India by Monk Faxian

(*Faxian zhuan*, T51n2085_001.0863a14),[11] indicates that there are two periods of the summer retreat in a year, the former summer retreat (*qian anju*) and the latter summer retreat (*hou anju*), with the former covering the period from the sixteenth day of the fourth month to the fifteenth day of the seventh month and the later from the sixteenth day of the fifth month to the fifteenth day of the eighth month (*Mohe sengqi lü*, T22n1425_027.0451b06). Notably, the monastic principles and precepts set in this Vinaya text were all 'those observed by the First Great Saṃgha (*dazhong*) when the Buddha was still in the world' (*Faxian zhuan*, T51n2085_001.0863a14), and it is for this reason, among others, that Faxian decided to translate it shortly after he returned to China (Zhan 2019).

During the retreat, monks and nuns stay in their monasteries for intensive meditation – a common practice among Buddhist communities in ancient India that is still observed in East and Southeast Asia, particularly by Thervadāda practitioners (Figure 4.3). Starting from the fifteenth day of the fourth month, the summer retreat runs over ninety days up to the fifteenth day of the seventh month, a day also called 'Qiyue ban' ('Mid-Seventh Month') in

Figure 4.3 Thai monks and lay practitioners at Vassa. Photo courtesy of Phra Kiattisak Kittipanyo.

11 The other two Vinaya texts are the *Monastic Rules of the Sarvāstivādin Schoo* (Skr. *Sarvāstivādin vinaya*; Ch. *Sapoduozhong lü*, which is better known as *Shisong lü* or *Monastic Rules in Ten Recitations*) and the *Monastic Rules of the Mahīśāsaka School in Five Divisions* (Skr. *Mahīśāsaka vinaya*; Ch. *Mishasai wufen lü*).

Chinese Buddhism, as described in the *Commentary on Practices and Matters in the* Monastic Rules in Four Divisions, *by Deleting the Complex and Supplementing the Missing* (Sifenlü *shanfan buque xingshi chao*, T40n1804_001.0038a03), a Vinaya text composed by the eminent monk of the Tang dynasty, Daoxuan (596–667).

The summer retreat is usually concluded with a confession ceremony called Pravāraṇa (*zizi*) (Figure 4.4), in which monastics each come before the Saṃgha to confess and atone for an offence they have made during the retreat, the rules and regulations of which are set out in detail in such Vinaya classics as the *Monastic Rules in Four Divisions* (*Sifen lü*, T22n1428–037–038) of the Dharmaguptaka school, the *Monastic Rules in Ten Recitations* (*Shisong lü*, T23n1435_024) of the Sarvāstivāda school and the *Monastic Rules of the Great Saṃgha School* (*Mohe sengqi lü*, T22n1425_027).

What is of particular interest to us is a ritual, which is mentioned more than once in the *Record of Buddhist Kingdoms*, of making offerings (*gongyang*) to the Saṃgha at the close of the summer retreat that had been performed in association with the Pravāraṇa Ceremony for centuries across Central and South Asia. When recalling his short stay in the Central Asian kingdom of Jiecha (modern Tashi Ku'ergan in Xinjiang), Faxian notes an annual ceremony of offering ripened wheat to Buddhist monks upon their return from the summer retreat (*Faxian zhuan*, T51n2085_001.0857a06).

Figure 4.4 Pavāraṇā Ceremony at Wat Phra Dhammakaya, Khlong Luang District, Pathum Thani Province, Thailand. Photo courtesy of Phra Kiattisak Kittipanyo.

Faxian (aka Fâ-Hien 2019) also gives a fairly detailed account of a grand offering ceremony performed after the summer retreat throughout India:

> Where a community of monks resides, they erect topes to Sariputtra, to Maha-maudgalyayana, and to Ānanda, and also topes (in honour) of the Abhidharma, the Vinaya, and the Sutras. A month[12] after the (annual season of) rest [*anju yi yue*], the families which are looking out for blessing stimulate one another to make offerings to the monks and send round to them the liquid food which may be taken out of the ordinary hours. All the monks come together in a great assembly and preach the Law; after which offerings are presented at the tope of Sariputtra, with all kinds of flowers and incense. All through the night lamps are kept burning, and skilful musicians are employed to perform. When Sariputtra was a great Brahman, he went to Buddha, and begged (to be permitted to quit his family (and become a monk). The great Mugalan [Damulian] and the great Kasyaal [Dajiaye] also did the same.[13]
>
> When the monks have done receiving their annual tribute (from the harvests) [*shousui*], the Heads of the Vaisyas and all the Brahmans bring clothes and other such articles as the monks require for use and distribute among them. The monks, having received them, also proceed to give portions to one another. From the nirvana of Buddha, the forms of ceremony, laws, and rules, practised by the sacred communities, have been handed down from one generation to another without interruption.

Faxian describes the ritual of offering sacrifices to the Saṃgha as a widespread annual event that took place after the summer retreat. Although he does not mention the exact date(s) of the annual ceremony, his description of the sacrificial ritual performed at the stupas of Śāriputra, Ānanda and particularly Maudgalyāyana to the accompaniment of music presents valuable historical evidence for this centuries-old Indian tradition.

12 I suspect that the Chinese character *yue* for 'month' as shown here in the English translation is a corruption of the Chinese character *ri* for 'day'.

13 A more plausible reading of the unpunctuated sentence(s) in the original text of Chinese, *shi jiyue ren zuo Shelifu da Poluomen shi yi Fo qiu chujia Damulian Dajiaye yi ru shi* (*Faxian zhuan*, T51n2085_001.0858a11), should be: 'Entertainers are employed to enact [the story of] Śāriputra going to the Buddha to seek his permission to become a monk when he was a great Brahmin. [Stories about] Mahāmaudgalyāyana and Mahākāśyapa are likewise [enacted].' Accordingly, *zuo* ('to act'; 'to enact') in the phrase *shi jiyue ren zuo* is to be understood as a transitive verb that takes the clause *Shelifu da Poluomen shi yi Fo qiu chujia* as its object.

A more detailed record of the annual post-Vārsika ritual of sacrifice to the Buddha and the Saṃgha in ancient India is found in *Xuanzang*'s *Great Tang Record of Journeys to the Western Regions* (*Xiyu ji*, T51n2087_008.0918c13), as shown below:[14]

> Every year when the Bhikṣus release themselves from the summer retreat, religious persons and lay persons of the four quarters come together in thousands and myriads. During seven days and nights, they scatter flowers, burn incense and sound music as they parade through the communities and pay their worship and present offerings. The priests of India, according to the holy instruction of the Buddha, on the first day of the first half of the month Śrâvana enters on Vārsika. With us this is the sixteenth day of the fifth month; they give up their retreat on the fifteenth day of the second half of the month Âśvayuja, which is with us the fifteenth day of the eighth month.

Aśvayuja (Ch. *anshifuyushe*), according to Monk Xuanzang (*Xiyu ji*, T51n2087_002. 0875c15; see also Fouw and Svoboda 2003: 185), is the first month of autumn in the Hindu lunar calendar, which corresponds to the period from the sixteenth day of the seventh month till the fifteenth day of the eighth month with the first fortnight of the month (waxing cycle) from the New Moon to the Full Moon called 'the white portion' (*Śukla Paksha*) and the second fortnight of the month (waning cycle) from the Full Moon back to the New Moon called the 'dark portion' (*Kṛiṣhṇa Paksha*). The Tang dynasty monk also notes in his travel record (*Xiyu ji*, T51n2087_002.0875c15):

> In India, the name of the months depends on the stars, and from ancient days till now, there has been no change in this. But as the different schools have translated the accounts according to the dialects of the countries without distinguishing one from the other, mistakes have arisen. As a consequence, contradictions are apparent in the division of the seasons. Hence it is in some places they enter on Vārsika on the sixteenth day of the fourth month and break up on the fifteenth day of the seventh month.

From the above description, it is possible for us to draw the following inferences:

(1) The annual ritual of sacrifice at the end of the summer retreat to the Saṃgha is a Buddhist ceremony closely connected with the Pavāraṇā Ceremony, observed all over India since the time of the historical Buddha;

14 The passage is translated with a minor modification to Beal (1904: 135–136).

(2) The ritual lasts for seven days and seven nights;
(3) The ritual involves both the clergy (*fa*) and the laity (*su*) gathering together, scattering flowers, burning incense, performing music and parading through villages and towns;
(4) The specific dates of the ritual vary somewhat from place to place, the earlier one falling on the fifteenth day of the seventh month and the later one on the fifteenth day of the eighth month.

Faxian and Xuanzang's accounts of the Pavāraṇā Ceremony and sacrificial ritual held at the close of the summer retreat in Central and South Asia are corroborated by Monk Yijing (635–713) in his *Record of the Buddhist Religion: As Practised in India and the Malay Archipelago* (*Nanhai jigui neifa zhuan*, T54n2125; hereafter cited as *Neifa zhuan*) – a travelogue of his twenty-five-year sojourn in Srivijava (modern Palembang of Sumatra in Indonesia) and India. In Chapter XIV on 'The Summer-Retreat of the Five Parishads' ('Wuzhong anju') (*Neifa zhuan*, T54n2125_002.0217a25), Yijing (aka I-Tsing 1896: 85) writes: 'On the day on which the summer-retreat closes, priests and laymen perform a great ceremony of offering (Pûgâ) [...], the day on which the *kaṭhina* robes are spread out (as a present to the Saṃgha), which is an ancient custom.' In the following chapter 'Concerning the Pravârana-Day' ('Suiyi chenggui') (*Neifa zhuan*, T54n2125_002.0217b20–0217c10), Yijing goes on to describe at greater length a wide range of ritual performances held by Buddhist priests and lay devotees from gathering in a great assembly on the night of the fourteenth day to listen to a precentor preaching a Buddhist sūtra from a high seat to lighting lamps and offering incense and flowers to the Buddha and the Saṃgha, to hoisting banners and setting up canopies on the morning of the fifteenth day, to bringing storeyed carriages, carrying images in sedan chairs and parading through towns and villages until the forenoon, to all returning to the monastery to hold the Great Fast or Upavasatha (*dazhai*) at noon and gathering together again in the afternoon to perform the *Pravāraṇā* (*suiyi*) Ceremony to confess and repent of sins, and to laymen presenting gifts and alms before the assembly and the Saṃgha distributing them among its members in the evening.

The three-month summer retreat concludes with the Pravāraṇā Ceremony, which is in turn followed by a ritual of offering gifts and alms by lay devotees to the Saṃgha as described above by Yijing. This ritual is commonly referred to in the Vinaya *as kaṭhina* or as *jiachinayi/jianguyi* in the Chinese translation of scriptures on monastic rules and regulations such as the *Vinaya mātṛkā* (*Pinimu jing*, T24n1463_002.0807b29, T24n1463_003.0815a13–18) and the *Mahīśāsaka vinaya* (*Mishasaibu hexi wufen lü*, T22n1421_004.0023b01–0023b29). The word *kaṭhina*, meaning 'robe' and 'cotton cloth' when used as a noun and 'rough' and 'hard' when used as an adjective in Sanskrit and

Figure 4.5 Kaṭhina Ceremony, Chaiyaphum Province, Thailand. Photo courtesy of Phra Kiattisak Kittipanyo.

Pāli, is understood as a rubric name for the kaṭhina robe offering festival – a living tradition that started to be observed at the time of the Buddha and has continued to be performed in various forms into the twenty-first century in Theravāda Buddhist countries such as Sri Lanka, Laos, Cambodia, Myanmar and Thailand (Figure 4.5), although the day for celebrating the festival varies from place to place due to different dates of entering the summer retreat (Holt 2017: 140–173).

In medieval China, Buddhists held the Kaṭhina Ceremony on the fifteenth day of the seventh month (Chang 1957; Chen 1983: 74; Chen 1999: 241; Wu 2001: 38–44). In his study of the Yulanpen Festival in relation to the Chinese tradition of ancestor worship, Xing (2011: 126) identifies the *Pravāraṇa Sūtra* (*Shou xinsui jing*, T01n0061) as 'the earliest Chinese translation of sūtra that records the fifteenth day of the seventh month on lunar calendar as the day for the *Kaṭhina* ceremony'.[15] More scriptural evidence for the fifteenth day of the seventh

15 It is worth noting, however, that no record of the *Shou xinsui jing* is found in any Buddhist catalogues from early and medieval China, although the text is included in the Khitan Buddhist Canon (*Danzang*), the Song Buddhist Canon (*Songzang*) and the Taishō Tripiṭaka, where Dharmarakṣa is given as the translator. So we are not very certain as to whether it was translated by Dharmarakṣa, or if not, who translated it and when, nor are we certain as to whether this is 'the earliest Chinese translation of sūtra that records the fifteenth day of the seventh month on lunar calendar as the day for the Kaṭhina ceremony', as stated in Xing (2011: 126).

month as the day for holding the Pravāranā Ceremony and the Kaṭhina Ritual can be found in the *Separate Translation of Saṃyuktāgama* (*Bieyi za ahan jing*, T02n0100_012.0457a29), a shorter Chinese version of the *Saṃyuktāgama* (*Za ahan jing*, T02n0099) that has been convincingly dated to fall between 385 and 431 by Mizuno (1970: 45, quoted in Bingenheimer 2011: 1), and also in the *Ekottarika āgama* (*Zengyi ahang jing*, T02n0125_024.0676b29), which was translated into Chinese by Gautama Saṃghadeva (Ch. Qutan Sengjiatipo) in 397. In the section on 'Merit Accumulation' ('Shanju'), the *Ekottarika āgama* records an instruction to Ānanda from the Buddha: 'Now you are out in the open air, you should strike the bell (*jianzhui*) without delay. This is because today is the fifteenth day of the seventh month – a day for *shousui*' (ibid.).

The ritual of *shousui* (lit. 'to receive one year of age') is also called in Chinese *shoula*, meaning 'to receive offerings at the end of summer retreat'. Under the entry for 'Making Offerings at the End of Summer Retreat' ('Ci xiala') in *A Brief History of the Saṃgha Compiled in the Great Song* (*Da Song seng shilüe*, T54n2126_003.0251a06; hereafter cited as *Seng shilüe*), Monk Zanning (919–1001), a prominent Vinaya scholar, states:

> With respect to *la*, the sixteenth day of the seventh month is designated in the sūtra and vinayas as New Year's Day (*suishou*) for the Five-part Dharma-body (*wufen fashen*) of bhikṣus. The fifteenth day of the seventh month is thus the Eve of the End-of-Summer Retreat Offering (*lachu*). The ordination age of bhikṣus is not calculated according to any secular calendar but decided by the number of summer retreats [one has completed]. The sūtras and vinayas also call the fifteenth day [of the seventh month] 'the Day for Making Offerings to the Buddhist (*fo la ri*)'.

For Buddhist monks and nuns, the Pravāraṇā Ceremony marks the end of an old year, whereas the Kaṭhina Ceremony the beginning of a new year, because the completion of an annual summer retreat means to them a one-year increase in their 'dharma age' (*fala*) or 'ordination age' (*jiela*), as promulgated in the *Essential Readings for Buddhists* (*Shishi yaolan*, T54n2147_003.0298c29).

Significantly, Yijing in his travel record makes a point of performing the ritual on the fifteenth day of the seventh month of carrying images in sedan chairs and parading through villages and towns while drumming, dancing and presenting music performances all the way being the same as what was called in the Divine Land (Shenzhou, i.e. China) the 'ceremony of parading round a city (*xingcheng fa*)' (*Neifa zhuan*, T54n2125_002.0217b20; see also I-Tsing 1896: 87). The parading-round-the-city ceremony observed by Yijing in South and Southeast Asia is better known in China as 'parading the image of the Buddha through the city' (*xuncheng*) or 'carrying the image of the Buddha in procession' (*xingxiang*). In *A Brief History of the Saṃgha Compiled in the Great Song* (*Seng shilüe*, T54n2126_001.0237a25), Zanning describes *xuncheng* and *xingxiang* as a grand ritual performance that is held 'in every [Buddhist] country', a ritual that involves carrying the Buddha's image in a five-storeyed pagoda-like wagon and parading it through a city, and he also notes that this ceremony is performed in the Native Land of Xia (Tuxia, i.e. China) as well at the close of the summer retreat with 'monks and lay people marching in two columns while holding flowers and fans, and blowing seashell horns and sounding cymbals – [a ritual performance] called "filing out for Kaṭhina" (*chudui jiati*) because it is held in the month of Kaṭhina (*jiati yue*)'.

It is clear from the travel and historical records by the eminent monks that the Yulanpen Festival is not a Chinese creation but an ancient Indian tradition with its origin in the Kaṭhina Ceremony that is performed in association with the Pravāranā Ceremony.

Similar accounts of the fifteenth day of the seventh month as a day for making offerings to the Saṃgha are also found in a genre of strange writings known as *zhiguai* ('accounts of the strange') prevalent during the Six Dynasties (AD 220–589). Notable among them is the *Signs from the Unseen Realm* (*Mingxiang ji*, 276–343; Campany 2012: 63–260), which, compiled around 490 by Wang Yan (b. ca. 454), is the most representative and the largest collection of Buddhist miracle tales from early medieval China. Included in it is a story about Monk Huida being raised from the dead by Bodhisattva Avalokiteśvara or Guanshiyin after expounding the Dharma to him.[16] The bodhisattva concludes his preaching by saying:

> Whenever one acts so as to establish fortune for the departed, whether they be one's parents, siblings, relatives of up to seven generations ago, relatives by marriage, friends, or passers-by, whether done in an oratory or in the home, whoever among those departed may be suffering will be released. On the fifteenth day of the seventh month, monks receive end-of-retreat offerings; to present offerings at this time is most effective. If one provides vessels and fills them with offering foods, with each dish labeled 'such-and-such a person personally presents this to the three treasures,' the fortune dispensed thereby will be especially great, and the recipients' felicity will be greater and faster. (Campany 2012: 150)

Guanshiyin's lecture on the Dharma is closely comparable to the instruction the Buddha gives to Maudgalyāyana in the *Yulanpen Sūtra* on performing

16 The *Signs from the Unseen Realm* fails to survive in its original form. What remains of this *zhiguai* work is a reconstructed text by Lu Xun (1881–1936), who gleaned this story from the *Pearl Grove in the Dharma Garden* (*Fayuan zhulin*, T53n2122_086.0919b20), a seventh-century Buddhist encyclopaedia compiled by Monk Daoshi (d. 683).

the ritual of offering Yulan bowls to the Buddha and the Saṃgha on the fifteenth day of the seventh month. Monk Huida (fl. 375) is known also by his secular name as Liu Sahe, a historical figure of the Eastern Jin dynasty (*Gaoseng zhuan*, T50n2059_013.0409b13; see also Zhang 1985: 154), who accompanied Faxian along with nine other monk scholars on his pilgrimage to India (*Faxian zhuan*, T51n2085_001.0857a06–0858a1). The mention in this *zhiguai* story of the fifteenth day of the seventh month as a day for monks to 'receive end-of-retreat offering' is a very valuable piece of evidence to corroborate Faxian's account of the aforementioned Lafo Ceremony held on the fifteenth day of the seventh month in Qingzhou in the early fifth century.

Yulanpen Festival vs. Zhongyuan Festival

'Which came first, the Buddhist Yulanpen Festival or the Daoist Zhongyuan Festival?' This question has always been among the most contentious issues concerning the debate and discussion on the authenticity of the *Yulanpen Sūtra*. For example, in arguing against the authenticity of the *Yulanpen Sūtra*, Zhu (1993: 8) insists that the fifteenth day of the seventh month designated by the Buddha in the sūtra as the Day of the Buddha's Delight, the Pravāraṇā Day when the Buddha's disciples and followers are supposed to place food and fruit in bowls and offer them up to the Saṃgha so as to receive Buddhist blessings on their current parents and ancestors of the past seven generations is 'actually the Middle-Primordial (Zhongyuan) Day, which is a holy day in Daoism for offering sacrifices to "the Officer of Earth Who Forgives Sins" '. Zhu does not think of it as a sheer coincidence that the Yulanpen Festival falls on the same day as the Zhongyuan Festival, contending that Chinese Buddhists designated the Daoist Zhongyuan Day for celebrating the Yulanpen Festival in order to offset Daoist influence and enhance Buddhist influence.

Hsiao (1995: 231–251; 1996: 84–85; 2005: 327–328) goes to the extreme of suspicion in this regard, asserting – despite evidence to the contrary – that there was no such religious practice in India as offering sacrifices to the Buddha and the Saṃgha on the fifteenth day of the seventh month and that the Yulanpen Festival was modelled after the Zhongyuan Festival, particularly its Ceremony of Great Offerings (*daxian*). Like many other researchers on the origin of the Zhongyuan/Yulanpen Festival, Hsiao also notes that the *Yulanpen Sūtra* is similar in theme and content to a Daoist scripture included in the *Daoist Canon Compiled During the Reign Period of Zhengtong* (*Zhengtong Daozang*) under the title of the *Scripture of the Supreme Numinous Treasure of Pervasive Mystery on the Great Offerings Made to the Three Primes of the Jade Capital Mountain in the Mysterious Metropolis* (*Taishang dongxuan lingbao sanyuan yujing xuandu daxian jing*, DZ 370; hereafter *Scripture on the Great Offerings*), a one-scroll text which is held in high regard by Daoists as the scriptural source for the Zhongyuan Festival. The similarity between them leads Hsiao to believe that the *Yulanpen Sūtra* was composed by Chinese Buddhists in imitation of the *Scripture on the Great Offerings*.

As suggested by its title, the *Scripture on the Great Offerings* is a Daoist scripture of the Numinous Treasure (*lingbao*) School. Its original text, datable to the late Six Dynasties (220–589), fails to survive intact. No mention of this Daoist scripture has been found in any extant pre-Tang Daoist sources. The earliest known reference to it appears in the *Classified Collection of Arts and Letters* (*Yiwen leiju* 4.80), an early Tang category book (*leishu*) or encyclopaedia compiled in 624 by Ouyang Xun (557–641), who quotes the following for the entry of 'Zhongyuan Festival' from a certain Daoist text called *Daojing* (*Scripture of the Way*):[17]

> The *Daojing* says: the fifteenth day of the seventh month is the Middle Primordial Day. The Officer of Earth checks his figures, searching through the human world to distinguish good from evil. All of the gods and assembled sages arrive together at the palace to calculate the kalpas and numbers and check human or ghosts' registers, and hungry ghosts and prisoners all converge at once. On this day, the Great Offering of the Mysterious Metropolis (*xuandu daxian*) should be made to the Jade Capital Mountain: select myriad flowers and fruits, precious gems and rare items, banners and jewelled vessels, delicacies and food, and offer them to all of the assembled sages. All day and all night, Daoist priests should preach and chant this scripture, and great sages of the Ten Directions should sing together from its numinous pages. All of the prisoners and hungry ghosts can eat their fill, completely escape from suffering, and come back among humans.[18]

The Great Offering of the Mysterious Metropolis held on the Zhongyuan Day shows striking resemblance to the Yulanpen Ceremony as described in the *Yulanpen Sūtra*. This gives rise to a question as to which of them

17 A slightly different version of this quote appears in the *Materials for Early Learning* (*Chuxue ji* 4. 79), compiled around 720 in imitation of the *Classified Collection of Arts and Letters* by Xu Jian (660–729), who follows Ouyang Xun by giving the *Daojing* as the source for the entry of 'Zhongyuan Festival'. The so-called *Daojing* has been convincingly identified as the *Daxian jing* or *Scripture on the Great Offerings* – a point I will return to later in this chapter with more details.

18 The translation is primarily based on Teiser (1988: 36), which is quoted with some minor modifications in Lü (2011: 51).

came first, the *Yulanpen Sūtra*/Yulanpen Festival or the *Scripture on the Great Offerings*/Zhongyuan Festival. As early as the Tang dynasty, Monk Falin (572–640), a Buddhist apologist, declares stoutly in his *Defending the Rightful* (*Bianzheng lun*, T52n2110_008.0548a02) that the fifteenth day of the seventh month is not a Daoist festival, which is echoed by Monk Xuanyi (fl. 684–704) in his *Determining the Rightful* (*Zhenzheng lun*, T52n2112_003.0569c04):

> Since the Tang, [...] there have been Daoist priests such as Li Xing from Yizhou and Fang Zhang of Lizhou who co-forged the *Scripture on the Sea-like Emptiness* (*Haikong jing*)[19] in ten scrolls, Li Rong who forged the *Scripture on Ritual Bathing* (*Xiyu jing*) in response to the *Bathhouse* (*Wenshi*),[20] and Liu Wudai who forged the *Scripture on the Great Offerings* in imitation of the *Yulanpen Sūtra*.

Their assumption about the influence of the *Yulanpen Sūtra*/Yulanpen Festival on the *Scripture on the Great Offerings*/Zhongyuan Festival has been widely accepted as true by modern scholars of Chinese religion (e.g. Akizuki 1961 and 1965; Yoshioka 1970; Ōfuchi 1985; Chen 1987; Tesier 1988: 35–38; Wu 2001: 120–129; Kohn 2009: 54–55; Lü 2011) with the notable exception of Hsiao (1995, 1996 and 2005).

Hsiao (1995: 242) strongly 'suspects that the *Yulanpen Sūtra* was copied from the *Scripture on the Great Offerings*', but he fails to produce any evidence from pre-Tang sources except the above-mentioned entry for the Zhongyuan Festival in the seventh-century encyclopaedia, *Classified Collection of Arts and Letters*. Despite the fact that all the evidence available to him suggests the opposite, Hsiao (1995: 242) still holds on to his belief, arguing:

> In terms of content, part of this scripture [i.e. the *Scripture on the Great Offerings*] shows Buddhist influence, but even if the time when the composition of this scripture was completed had not been necessarily earlier than that of Dharmarakṣa's *Yulanpen Sūtra*, [...] and even if Dharmarakṣa had not copied this scripture, his [*Yulanpen Sūtra*] must have been copied from some earlier Daoist scripture(s) on Zhongyuan.

---

19 The full title of this Daoist text is *The Grand Supreme Scripture on the Sea-like Emptiness and Storehouse of Wisdom on One Vehicle* (*Taishang yicheng haikong zhizang jing*, DZ 9).

20 Here, the *Bathroom* is an abbreviation of the *Sūtra Expounded by the Buddha on Bathing the Saṃgha in the Bathhouse* (*Fo shuo wenshi xiyu zhongseng jing*, T16n0701).

The absurdity of this argument is self-evident, and the greater absurdity is the reason Hsiao (1995: 242) gives to support his above claim:

> All the Daoist scriptures about Zhongyuan in the Daoist Canon are concerned with dispelling disasters and redeeming [sinners] and deal with the theme of rescuing the souls of the deceased, whereas Buddhism emphasises 'one saving oneself from the sins one has committed' (*ziye zijiu* [lit. 'self-karma and self-salvation']) rather than saving the souls of those already deceased.

Based on the one-sided interpretation of Buddhist salvation, Hsiao (1995: 242) insists that the *Yulanpen Sūtra* must have been copied from either the *Scripture on the Great Offerings* or some earlier Daoist scriptures on Zhongyuan. It is well known, however, among scholars of Chinese religion (e.g. Zürcher 1980: 134, 140, 143–144; Qing 1990: 160, 166–168; Bokenkamp 2008 and Xing 2012: 137–138) that ancient Lingbao scriptures were heavily influenced by Buddhism, particularly its Mahāyāna tradition and that the *gongyang* ritual of offering (Skr. *pūjā*), one of the oldest primary practices of Indian Buddhism (Buswell and Lopez 2013: 679), was incorporated into the Lingbao scriptures in the late fifth century at the earliest and transformed from offering to the Buddhist Triple Jewel (the Buddha, the Dharma and the Saṃgha) (Ch. *gongyang sanbao*; Skr. *ratnatraya pūjā*) into offering to the Daoist Triple Jewel (the Dao, the Scripture and the Master) (Lü 2011: 59). The influence of Buddhism on Daoism also manifests itself in the *Scripture on the Great Peace* (*Taiping jing*, DZ 1101), one of the earliest scriptures in the Daoist religious tradition with parts of the text datable to the second century AD (Tang 1983; 2006). In describing Buddhist salvation as an egocentric pursuit and using it as evidence against the authenticity of the *Yulanpen Sūtra*, here and once again, Hsiao ignores the fact that a number of popular Lingbao scriptures (e.g. DZ 1114; DZ 1115 and DZ 1205) associate Mahāyāna Buddhism with the altruistic pursuit of 'first save others and then save oneself' (*xian duren hou duji*) – a view widely held among Daoists in the Six Dynasties on Mahāyāna Buddhism, as noted by Zürcher (1980: 134–135).

Interestingly, Yoshioka (1970) does not deny the influence of the *Yulanpen Sūtra* on the *Scripture on the Great Offerings*, nor does he exclude the influence on the *Yulanpen Sūtra* of the *Scripture on the Precepts of the Three Primes* (*Sanyuan pinjie jing*), a Lingbao text datable to the mid- to late fourth century with a section on the 'measure of merits' (*gongde qingzhong*) later added to deal with ancestor worship in association with the Three Primes (Sanyuan) in Daoism. He (1970: 265–266, 277–279) believes that the idea of ancestor worship in the Three Primes – the Middle Prime (Zhongyuan) in particular – developed in the *Scripture on the Precepts of the Three Primes* forms the basis first of the Buddhist *Yulanpen Sūtra* and then of the *Scripture on the Great Offerings*, which was composed in imitation of the *Yulanpen Sūtra*. Accordingly, he (1970: 281) dates the *Yulanpen Sūtra* to fall between the late fourth and mid-fifth centuries, about fifty years later than the *Scripture on the Precepts of the Three Primes*. Clearly, Yoshioka looks at the *Yulanpen Sūtra* in relation to the *Scripture on the Great Offerings* from a perspective different from Hsiao, but he identifies the *Scripture of the Precepts of the Three Primes* as the source of inspiration for the *Yulanpen Sūtra* while ignoring the strong influence of Buddhism in Lingbao scriptures, thus demonstrating no fundamental difference from Hsiao in his view of the origin of the sūtra in Daoism.

Inevitably, the *Scripture on the Great Offerings* invites comparison with the *Yulanpen Sūtra*. By juxtaposing an incomplete text of the *Scripture on the Great Offerings* preserved in the Dunhuang manuscript numbered 3061 in the Pelliot Collection with a commentary version of this scripture in the *Daoist Canon Compiled During the Reign Period of Zhengtong* (*Zhengtong Daozang*, DZ 370), Chen Tsu-Lung (1987: 79), a renowned Dunhuang expert, confirms – beyond doubt – that the so-called *Daojing* or *Scripture of the Way* given in the *Classified Collection of Arts and Letters* (*Yiwen leiju* 4.80) as the source for the entry of 'Zhongyuan Festival' is none other than the *Scripture on the Great Offerings*, which, as mentioned before, is identified in the *Determining the Rightful* (*Zhenzheng lun*, T52n2112_003.0569c04) as forged by Liu Wudai in imitation of the *Yulanpen Sūtra*. Notably, Xuanyi (fl. 684–704), the author of the apologia, was himself an apostate who renounced Daoism to embrace Buddhism and also a compiler of the *Collated Catalogue of Collected Scriptures Compiled in the Great Zhou* (*Da Zhou mulu*, T55n2153), so we have every reason to believe that his description of the *Scripture on the Great Offerings* as a forgery of the *Yulanpen Sūtra* is very likely based on his firsthand knowledge and is therefore very reliable and valuable.[21]

In his ground-breaking study of the ghost festival in medieval China, Teiser (1988: 38) compares the *Scripture on the Great Offerings* with the *Yulanpen Sūtra*, finding that the former 'includes a parallel cast of characters as well as phrases employing the same locutions as the *Yü-lan-p'en Sūtra*'. Just as the Buddha instructs Maudgalyāyana in the *Yulanpen Sūtra* to make Yulanpen offerings to the Saṃgha so as for them to pray for the liberation of his mother from the Preta realm because it is beyond his power as a single individual to save Maudgalyāyana's mother, so does the Celestial Worthy of Primordial Commencement (Yuanshi tianzun) in the *Scripture on the Great Offerings*, where

21 For an informative study of the *Determining the Rightful* or *Zhenzheng lun* as a valuable source of Daoism in medieval China, see Palumbo (1997: 305–322, esp. 306, 318).

he tells the Supreme Sovereign of the Way (Taishang daojun) that the only way to liberate prisoners and hungry ghosts from suffering in the Earth Prison (*diyu*, a Chinese word for hell) is to make offerings on the fifteenth day of the seventh month to 'three generations of celestial worthies, myriad saints of the Ten Directions, seven generations of ancestors and nine generations of descendants (*jiuxuan qizu*) and all sentient beings in the Realm of Phenomena (*fajie cangsheng*)' in line with the 'Liturgies Regarding the Great Offering of the Mysterious Metropolis in the Jade Capital Mountain' ('Yujing xuandu daxian guiyi') because it is beyond his power as a single individual to deliver and exempt sinners from suffering in the Earth Prison (DZ 370: 1.12). All the evidence, internal and external, seems to suggest that the development of the Zhongyuan Festival was strongly influenced by Buddhism, not the other way around (Teiser 1988: 35).

Lü (2011: 58–60) reaffirms the widely held belief that medieval Daoist priests were inspired by the *Yulanpen Sūtra* to compose the *Scripture on the Great Offerings* and that the Great Offerings of the Middle-Primordial Festival (*Zhongyuan daxian*) was modelled on the Yulanpen Ceremony. Based on a most meticulous, fine-grained analysis of the text and the textual history of the *Scripture on the Great Offerings* and a painstakingly close comparison of the *Scripture on the Great Offerings* and its scattered citations with other relevant Daoist texts from medieval China, particularly ancient scriptures of the Lingbao School, Lü (2011: 49) concludes that the Zhongyuan Festival is not purely an indigenous religious festival but originates partly from Buddhism. Noteworthy is a piece of 'corroborative evidence' Lü (2011: 49) produces to support his argument that there is no mention of the three Daoist holy days – the Upper-Primordial Day (Shangyuan) or the fifteenth day of the first month, the Middle-Primordial Day (Zhongyuan) or the fifteenth day of the seventh month and the Lower-Primordial Day (Xiayuan) or the fifteenth day of the tenth month – is made in early Chinese texts on festival and seasonal periods including the chapter of 'Monthly Ordinances' ('Yueling') in the *Book of Rites* (*Liji*), a Confucian classic compiled by Dai Sheng during the reign of Emperor Xuan (Xuandi, r. 91–48 BC) of the Western Han dynasty, and the *Monthly Ordinances for the Four Classes of People* (*Simin yueling*), which was compiled by the Eastern Han scholar-official Cui Shi (ca. AD 103–ca.170).

CONCLUSION

As we have seen, there has been a great deal of debate and discussion on the origin(s) of the *Yulanpen Sūtra* and the meaning of the word, *yulan/yulanpen*. Because of no such sūtra or word found extant in Indic sources and also because of its stress on filial piety and ancestor worship, among others, the sūtra is now overwhelmingly viewed as an indigenous Chinese Buddhist text, although it has never been labelled as an apocryphal scripture in Chinese Buddhist catalogues. A critical review of the major arguments prevailing in modern scholarship against the authenticity of the sūtra and a close examination of extensive textual and contextual evidence concerning the *Yulanpen Sūtra* strongly suggest a conclusion – contrary to the popular view – that the *Yulanpen Sūtra* is not a Chinese Buddhist creation but most probably a Chinese creative translation. Although there is no extant story or sūtra in Indic sources known to us, the storyline and subject matter of the Mulian myth are first and foremost Indian as evidenced by numerous *Jātaka*, and particularly *Avadānaśataka* and *Petavatthu* stories in Indian Buddhist literature as well as in pre- and non-Buddhist classics such as the *Manusmṛti* and *Mahābhārata*.

The same may be said of the Yulanpen Festival on the fifteenth day of the seventh month. Rather than modelled on the Zhongyuan Festival, the Yulanpen Festival was directly inspired by the *Yulanpen Sūtra* with its roots going back to the Pravāraṇā/Kaṭhina Ceremony performed at the close of rainy-season (summer) retreat throughout the cultural sphere of Indian Buddhism, although there is no denying the absorption into it of ritual and religious elements from Daoism and Confucianism in its historical development from a Buddhist ritual of sacrifice to a popular ghost festival widely observed in the Sinitic world and beyond.

With regards to filial piety and ancestor worship that feature prominently in the *Yulanpen Sūtra*, they are not at all in conflict with Indian Buddhism but entirely in conformity with Indian religious practices that are traceable to the Vedic Age (ca. 1500–ca. 500 BC) and still observable in the rite of śrāddha, although they may not be so central to Buddhism as to Confucianism.

Last but not least, the occurrence in the *Yulanpen Sūtra* of the words and expressions that are found native to Chinese culture is actually a widespread phenomenon in early Chinese translations of Indian Buddhist texts. It is common practice to use culture-specific words and expressions in the target language to render terms and notions in the source language that find no easy equivalents in the target language. In the case of the *Yulanpen Sūtra* (as well as other early Chinese translations of Buddhist scriptures), the use of culture-dependent words and expressions serves a two-fold purpose: to achieve a culturally and linguistically dynamic or functional equivalence in the translated text, and more importantly, to localise the sūtra to make it more accessible and acceptable to Chinese people.

GLOSSARY

anju	安居
anju yi yue	安居一月
anshifuyushe	頞濕縛庾闍
An Shigao	安世高
An Wenhui	安文惠
baiguan	百官
Baiyunguan	白雲觀
baiyi	白衣
Baochang	寶唱
Bao'en fengpen jing	報恩奉盆經
Bao'en jing	報恩經
Bianji	辯機
bianwen	變文
bieben	別本
biqiu	比丘
bishou	筆受
Bo Faju	帛法巨
Bo Yuanxin	帛元信
Bosiliwang	波斯匿王
buxiao zhu zhongsheng	不孝諸眾生
chanding	禪定
Chang'an	長安
Changguang	長廣
chaolu	抄錄
chuanyan	傳言
chudui jiati	出隊迦提
chujia	出家
ci'ai	慈愛
Ci xiala	賜夏臘
cixiao	慈孝
Cui Shi	崔寔
Dacheng qixin lun	大乘起信論

Dacheng jing danyi	大乘經單譯
Dai Sheng	戴聖
Dajiaye	大迦葉
Da Ming sanzang shengjiao mulu	大明三藏聖教目錄
Damuganlian	大目幹連
Damujianlian	大目犍連
Damulian	大目連
Danzang	丹藏
Dao	道
Dao'an	道安
daochang	道場
Daojing	道經
daolitian	忉利天
daoren	道人
Daoshi	道世
daoshi	道士
Daoxuan	道宣
daoxuan	倒懸
daoyan	道眼
Dapen jingtu jing	大盆淨土經
Datong	大同
daxian	大獻
Daxingshan si	大興善寺
dazhai	大齋
dazhong	大眾
Dezong	德宗
diguan shizui	地官赦罪
Dingguangfo	定光佛
Dinglin	定林
diyu	地獄
Dizang pusa benyuan jing	地藏菩薩本願經.
Doubei	斗北
doushuaitian	兜率天
Du Gongzhan	杜公瞻
Dunhuang	敦煌
Dunhuang pusa	敦煌菩薩
egui	餓鬼
egui jie	餓鬼節
Egui pin	餓鬼品
en	恩
erjing tongben yiyi	二經同本異譯
fa	法

fajie cangsheng	法界蒼生
Fajing	法經
Faju	法炬
Fajuyu	法句喻
fala	法臘
Fali	法立
Falin	法琳
fanben	梵本
fangdeng	方等
Fang Zhang	方長
Faxian	法顯
fayan	法眼
Fayun	法雲
Fei Changfang	費長房
Fengting	楓亭
Foguo ji	佛國記
Fo huanxiri	佛歡喜日
Fo lari	佛臘日
Fo sheng daolitian wei mu shuofa	佛昇忉利天為母說法
Fo sheng daolitian wei mu shoufa jing	佛昇忉利天為母說法經
Fo shuo beitong suyuan jing	佛說背痛宿緣經
Fo shuo sishi'er zhang jing	佛說四十二章經
Futian	福田
Futuo	佛陀
Fotuobatuoluo	佛陀跋陀羅
Fotuo nishe wulanpona menzuoluo sudalan	佛陀你舍烏藍婆拏門佐羅素呾纜
Fozu tongji	佛祖統紀
Fumu enzhong jing	父母恩重經
Gihae	己亥
Gaowang Guanshiyin jing	高王觀世音經
Gaozuo	高座
gong	供
gongde qingzhong	功德輕重
Gongxian	鞏縣
gongyang	供養
gongyang sanbao	供養三寶
Goryeo	高麗
guan	灌
Guanla jing	灌臘經
Guanshiyin	觀世音
guhun yegui	孤魂野鬼

guijie	鬼節
Haikong jing	海空經
Hami	哈密
heshang	和尚
hou anju	後安居
huben	胡本
Huida	慧達
Huidi	惠帝
Huihuwen Mile huijian ji	回鶻文彌勒會見記
Huijiao	慧皎
jiachinayi	迦絺那衣
jiajie	假借
Jianchu	建初
jianzhui	揵椎
Jiang Mi	江泌
jianguyi	堅固衣
Jiankang	建康
Jianye	建鄴
jiati yue	迦提月
jie	劫
Jiecha	竭叉
jiela	戒臘
jielü	戒律
Jin	晉
jing	經
Jingling	竟陵
Jingtu Yulanpen jing	淨土盂蘭盆經
jingxin gongyang	敬心供養
Jin Wudi	晉武帝
jiu daoxuan	救倒懸
Jiumoluoshi	鳩摩羅什
jiuqi	救器
jiuxuan qizu	九玄七祖
jiu zui bao	九罪報
jixu qiuzhen youxu yusu	既須求真又須喻俗
juan	卷
Juezhe	覺者
Juezhe shuo jiu daoxuan qi jing	覺者說救倒懸器經
Julütuo	拘律陀
Kaihuang	開皇
Kaiyuan	開元
Kang Mengxiang	康孟詳

Kang Senghui	康僧會
Kang Shu	康殊
kouxuan Jinyu	口宣晉語
la	臘
lachu	臘除
lafo	臘佛
Laifu	萊菔/萊茯
laifu	萊菔/萊茯
Laifugen	萊茯根/萊菔根
Laoshan	嶗山
Laozi huahu jing	老子化胡經
leishu	類書
Liang	梁
Liang Wudi	梁武帝
Liji	禮記
lingbao	靈寶
Li Rong	李榮
liuqin	六親
Liu Sahe	劉薩荷
liushu	六書
liutong	六通
Liu Wudai	劉無待
Li Xing	黎興
Lizhou	澧州
Loutan jing	樓炭經
Luobo	蘿蔔
Luofu	蘿菔/羅茯
luofu	蘿菔/羅茯
Luofugen	蘿菔根/羅茯根
Luoyang	洛陽
Maming	馬鳴
menzuoluo	門左羅
menzuonang	門左囊
Mile huijian ji	彌勒會見記
Mingquan	明佺
Mishasai wufen lü	彌沙塞五分律
Muganlian	目幹連
Mohemuganlian	摩訶目幹連
Mohemujianlian	摩訶目犍連
Mujianlian	目犍連
Mulian	目連
Mulian jiumu	目連救母

Mulian weimu zaopen	目連為母造盆
Nanjing	南京
neidian	內典
nengren	能仁
nengru	能儒
Nie Daozhen	聶道真
Nie Chengyuan	聶承遠
nishe	你舍
Palman Daejanggyeong	八萬大藏經
pen	盆
penzuona	盆佐那
pin	品
pindao	貧道
Pinshawang	瓶沙王
pusa	菩薩
pusa shamen	菩薩沙門
Qi	齊
qian anju	前安居
Qige xing	七個星
Qingdao	青島
Qingti	青提
Qingyang guan	清陽觀
Qingzhou	青州
qishi fumu	七世父母
Qiyueban	七月半
Qutan Sengjiatipo	瞿曇僧伽提婆
ren	仁
Renshou	仁壽
ri	日
ru	儒
ru shi wo wen	如是我聞
ruzang	入藏
Ruzang lu	入藏錄
sangong	三公
sanjing tongben bieyi yiming	三經同本別譯異名
sanjing tongben chongchu	三經同本重出
sanjing tongben yichu	三經同本異出
sanjing tongben yiyi	三經同本異譯
sangmen	桑門/喪門
santu	三塗
Sanyuan	三元
Sanyuan pinjie jing	三元品戒經

Sapoduozhong lü	薩婆多眾律
Sengfa	僧法
Sengmin	僧旻
sengren	僧人
Sengyou	僧祐
shamen	沙門
shamenna	沙門那
Shandong	山東
shangen	善根
Shangyuan	上元
Shanju	善聚
shaqiemennang	沙迦懣囊
sheduo	捨墮
Shelifu	舍利弗
Shelifu zhuan	舍利弗傳
Shelizi	舍利子
sheluomonu	舍羅摩弩
shengwen	聲聞
Shengyue	聖月
Shenseng	神僧
Shenzhou	神州
Shidi pusa	十地菩薩
shi jiyue ren zuo Shelifu da Poluomen shi yi Fo qiu chujia Damulian Dajiayeyi ru shi	使伎樂人作舍利弗大婆羅門時詣佛求出家大目連大迦葉亦如是
Shilimi	尸梨蜜
shimonanu	室摩那弩
Shisong lü	十誦律
shiyi	失譯
shiyi zajing	失譯雜經
shoula	受臘
shousui	受歲
Simin yueling	四民月令
Si tianwang shen	四天王神
Song	宋
songxi	誦習
Songzang	宋藏
su	俗
sudalan	素呾纜
Sui	隋
suishou	歲首
suiyi	隨意

Suiyi chenggui	隨意成規
sujiang	俗講
suomen	娑門
suming	宿命
suxi mingshou	宿習冥授
Taishang daojun	太上道君
Taishag dongxuan lingbao sanyuan pinjie jing	太上洞玄靈寶三元品戒經
Taishō shinshu daizō kyō	大正新脩大藏經
taixue boshi	太學博士
Tang	唐
Tanjing	曇景
Tashi Ku'ergan	塔什庫爾干
Tianjian	天監
tianyan	天眼
tingwei	廷尉
tongben chongchu	同本重出
Tongtai si	同泰寺
Tuxia	土夏
waidao	外道
Wangshecheng	王舍城
Wangsheng tang	往生堂
Wang Yan	王琰
weijing	偽經
weizao	偽造
wen ru shi	聞如是
Wenshi	溫室
Wenxuan	文宣
Wenyuan	文渊
wo	我
Wudabu wai zhu chongyi jing	五大部外諸重譯經
Wudi	武帝
wufen fashen	五分法身
wulanpona	烏藍婆拏
wuwei	無為
Wu Zetian	武則天
Wuzhong anju	五眾安居
Xi'an	西安
xia anju	夏安居
xian duren hou duji	先度人後度己
Xiangmo jing	降魔經
Xianyou	仙游

xiao	孝
Xiaocheng jing chongfan	小乘經重翻
Xiaocheng jing dan chong fan ben bing yi youwu lu	小乘經單重翻本并譯有無錄
Xiaocheng xiuduoluo shiyi lu	小乘修多羅失譯錄
xiaolian	孝戀
xiaoshun	孝順
Xiao Ziliang	蕭子良
Xiayuan	下元
xiazuo	夏坐
Xi chongfu si	西崇福寺
xiemo	邪魔
Xiguo	西國
Ximing si	西明寺
xingcheng fa	行城法
xingxiang	行像
Xinji Angong yijing lu	新集安公疑經錄
Xinji xuzhuan shiyi zajing lu	新集續撰失譯雜經録
Xinji yijing weizhuan zalu	新集疑經僞撰雜錄
xiu	宿
Xiyu jing	洗浴經
xuncheng	巡城
Xuandi	宣帝
xuandu daxian	玄都大獻
Xuanyi	玄嶷
Xuanying	玄應
Xuanzang	玄奘
Yancong	彥琮
Yanqi	焉耆
ye	頁/業
Yichu	義楚
Yijing	義淨
yijing	疑經
yinyuan	因緣
yiwei jing	疑偽經
Yixi	義熙
Youduoluo	優多羅
Youduoluo mu jing	優多羅母經
Youduoluo mu zhui egui yuan	優多羅母墮餓鬼緣
you jing zhong shuo	有經中說
yuanjue	緣覺
Yuanshi tianzun	元始天尊

yue	月
Yufo chansi	玉佛禪寺
Yueling	月令
Yujia shidi lun	瑜伽師地論
Yujing xuandu daxian guiyi	玉京玄都大獻規儀
yulan	盂蘭
Yulan jing	盂蘭經
yulanpen	盂蘭盆
Yulanpen jie	盂蘭盆節
Yurong	遇榮
zajing	雜經
Zanning	贊寧
Zengzi	曾子
Zherong	柘榮
zhiguai	志怪
zizi	自恣
zizi ri	自恣日
Zhengtong daozang	正統道藏
Zhenyuan	貞元
Zhi Loujiachen	支婁迦讖
Zhipan	志磐
Zhi Qian	支謙
Zhisheng	智昇
zhongjian diyi	塚間第一
Zhongjing shiyi	眾經失譯
Zhongtu mingci	中土名詞
Zhongyuan	中元
Zhongyuan daxian	中元大獻
Zhongyuan fahui	中元法會
Zhongyuan jie	中元節
zhongzhi pian	終制篇
zhuandu	轉讀
zhubo	竹帛
Zhu Tanmoluocha	竺曇摩羅察
zhu shi zhi qi	貯食之器
ziye zijiu	自業自救
Zongli zhongjing mulu	綜理眾經目錄
Zongmi	宗密
zuo	作
zuochan	坐禪
zuoxia	坐夏

BIBLIOGRAPHY

Primary Sources (list by title)

Bannihuan hou guanla jing 般泥洹後灌臘經. Translated by Zhu Fahu 竺法護 (Dharmarakṣa, d. 308). T12n0391.

Bensheng jing 本生經. Translated by Wuxing 悟醒. N31n0018.

Bianzheng lun 辯正論. Composed by Falin 法琳 (572–640). T52n2110.

Bieyi za ahan jing 別譯雜阿含經. Translated by Anonymous (fl. 385–431). T02n0100.

Bimo shi Mulian jing 弊魔試目連經. Translated by Zhi Qian 支謙 (fl. third century). T01n0067.

Chang ahan jing 長阿含經. Translated by Fotuoyeshe 佛陀耶舍 (Buddhayaśas, fl. 401) and Zhu Fonian 竺佛念 (fl. 383). T01n0001.

Chu sanzang jiji 出三藏記集. Compiled by Sengyou 僧祐 (445–18). T55n2145.

Chuxue ji 初學記. Compiled by Xu Jian 徐堅 (660–729). Rept. in 2 vols, Beijing: Zhonghua shuju, 2004.

Da Song seng shi lue 大宋僧史略. Compiled by Zanning 贊寧 (919–1001). *T54n2126.*

Da Tang neidian lu 大唐內典錄. Compiled by Daoxuan 道宣 (596–667). T55n2149.

Da Tang xiyu ji 大唐西域記. Recorded by Xuanzang 玄奘 (602–664), edited by Bianji 辯機 (619–49). T51n2087.

Da zhidu lu 大智度論. Composed by Longshu pusa 龍樹菩薩 (Nāgārjuna Bodhisattva, ca. 150–ca. 250), translated by Jiumoluoshi 鳩摩羅什 (Kumārajīva, 344–413). T25n1509.

Da Zhou kanding zhongjing mulu 大周刊定眾經目錄. Compiled by Mingquan 明佺 (fl. 695) et al. T55n2153.

Da zhuangyan lun jing 大莊嚴論經. Composed by Maming 馬鳴 (Aśvaghoṣa, ca. 80–ca. 150), translated by Kumārajīva. T04n0201.

Egui baoying jing 餓鬼報應經. Translated by Anonymous (fl. 350–420). T17n0746.

Egui shi jing 餓鬼事經. Translated by Yun'an 雲庵. N28n0014.

Fanyi mingyi ji 翻譯名義集. Compiled by Fayun 法雲 (1088–1158). T54n2131.

Fayuan zhulin 法苑珠林. Compiled by Daoshi 道世 (d. 683). T53n2122.

Fenbie gongde lun 分別功德論. Translated by Anonymous (fl. mid- to late fifth century). T25n1507.

Fo sheng daolitian weimu shoufa jing 佛昇忉利天為母說法經. Translated by Dharmarakṣa (d. 308). T17n0815.

Fo shuo bao'en fengpen jing 佛說報恩奉盆經. Translated by Anonymous during the Eastern Jin dynasty (317–420). T16n0686.

Fo shuo gui wen Mulian jing 佛說鬼問目連經. Translated by An Shigao 安世高 (ca. 148–180). T17n0734.

Fo shuo Mulian suo wen jing 佛說目連所問經. Translated by Fatian 法天 (Dharmadeva, d. 1001). T24n1468.

Fo shuo Mulian wen jieluü zhong wubai qingzhong shi 佛說目連問戒律中五百輕重事. Translated by Anonymous during the Eastern Jin dynasty (317–420). T24n1483a.

Fo shuo Mulian wen jielü zhong wubai qingzhong shi jing 佛說目連問戒律中五百輕重事經. Translated by Anonymous during the Eastern Jin dynasty (317–420). T24n1483b.

Fo shuo Mulian wen jieluü zhong wubai qingzhong shi jing shi 佛說目連問戒律中五百輕重事經釋. Ttranslated by Anonymous during the Eastern Jin dynasty (317–420). X44n0751.

Fo shuo Mulian wubai wen jing lü jie 佛說目連五百問經略解. Translated by Anonymous during the Eastern Jin dynasty (317–420). X44n0750.

Fo shuo wenshi xiyu zhongseng jing 佛說溫室洗浴眾僧經. Translated by An Shigao安世高 (ca. 148–180). T16n0701.

Fo shuo xingqi xing jing 佛說興起行經. Translated by Kang Mengxiang 康孟祥 (fl. AD 194). T04n0197.

Fo shuo Yulanpen jing 佛說盂蘭盆經. Translated by Dharmarakṣa (d. 308). T16n0685.

Fozu tongji 佛祖統紀. Compiled by Zhipan 志磐 (1220–1275). T49n2035.

Fu Fazang yinyuan zhuan 付法藏因緣傳. Translated by Jijiaye 吉迦夜 (Kiṃkārya) and Tanyao 曇曜 around the mid-fifth century. T50n2058.

Gaoseng Faxian zhuan 高僧法顯傳. Composed by Faxian 法顯 (ca. 337–422). T51n2085.

Gaoseng zhuan 高僧傳. Compiled by Huijiao惠皎 (497–554). T50n2059.

Genbenshuo yiqieyou bu pinaiye zashi 根本說一切有部毘奈耶雜事 703. Translated by Yijing 義淨 (635–713). T24n1451.

Guoqu xianzai yinguo jing 過去現在因果經. Translated by Qiunabatuoluo 求那跋陀羅 (Guṇabhadra, 394–468). T03n0189.

Jing-Chu suishi ji 荊楚歲時記. Zong Lin 宗懔 (ca. 498–565). In *Siku quanshu* 四庫全書, edited by Ji Yun 紀昀 (1724–1805), et al. Rept. in 1,500 vols. Taibei: Shangwu Yinshuguan, 1983–1986.

Jinglü yixang 經略異相. Compiled by Baochang 寶唱 (ca. 495–528) et al. T53n2121.

Jingtu yulanpen jing 淨土盂蘭盆經. Composed by Anonymous (fl. 600–650). Pelliot MS no. 2185 of the Fonds Pelliot Chinois. Paris: Bibliothèque Nationale, n.d. https://gallica.bnf.fr/ark:/12148/btv1b83018019.image#.

Kaiyuan Shijiao lu 開元釋教錄. Compiled by Zhisheng 智昇 (fl. 730). T55n2154.

Lidai Sanbao ji 歷代三寶記. Compiled by Fei Changfang 費長房 (fl. 581–618). T49n2034.

Lunyu zhushu 論語注疏. 1815. Commentated by He Yan 何晏 (d. AD 249), sub-commentated by Xing Bing 邢昺 (932–1010). In *Shisan jing zhushu* 十三經注疏, edited by Ruan Yuan 阮元 (1764–1849). Compact ed. in 2 vols. Beijing: Zhonghua shuju, 1980.

Lüshi chunqiu 呂氏春秋. 1782. Compiled by Lü Buwei 呂不韋 (d. AD 235). *Siku quanshu* ed.

Mingxiang ji 冥祥記. 1997. Compiled by Wang Yan 王琰 (b. ca. 454). In *Gu xiaoshuo gouchen* 古小說鉤沈, edited by Lu Xun 魯迅, 276–343. Rept. in separately published ed. Jinan: Qilu shushe.

Mishasaibu hexi wufen lü 彌沙塞部和醯五律分. Translated by Fotuoshi 佛陀什 (Buddhajīva, fl. mid- to late fifth century), Zhu Daosheng 竺道生 (355–434) and others. T22n1421.

Mohemoye jing 摩訶摩耶經. Translated by Tanjing 曇景 (fl. 479–502). T12n0383.

Mohe sengqi lü 摩訶僧祇律. Translated by Faxian 法顯 (337–422) and Fotuobatuoluo 佛陀跋陀羅 (Buddhabhadra, 359–423). T22n1425.

Mo raoluan jing 魔嬈亂經. Translated by Anonymous during the Eastern Jin dynasty (317–420). T01n0066.

Mozi xiangu 墨子閒詁. Written by Sun Yirang 孫詒讓 (1848–1908), edited and punctuated by Sun Qizhi 孫啟治. *Xinbian zhuzi jicheng* 新編諸子集成 ed. Beijing: Zhonghua shuju, 2001.

Nanhai jigui neifa zhuan 南海寄歸內法傳. Composed by Yijing 義淨 (635–713). T54n2125

Pinimu jing 毘尼母經. Translated by Anonymous (fl. late fourth century or early fifth century). T24n1463.

Qădimqi Uighur Yezighidiki Maitrı Simit. Hand-copied by Anonymous (fl. ca. ninth century). Edited by Israpil Yüsüp et al. Ürümchi: Shinjang Khălq Năshriyati, 1988.

Santian neijie jing 三天內解經. Composed by Santian dizi Xushi 三天弟子徐氏 (fl. mid-fifth century).DZ 1205.

Shisan jing zhushu 十三經注疏. 1815. Edited by Ruan Yuan 阮元 (1764–1849). Compact ed. in 2 vols. Beijing: Zhonghua shuju, 1980.

Shishi yaolan 釋氏要覽. Compiled by Daocheng 道誠 (fl. 998–1007). T54n2127.

Shisong lü 十誦律. Translated by Foruoduoluo 弗若多羅 (Puṇyatāra, fl. 404) and Jiumoluoshi 鸠摩罗什 (Kumārajīva, 344–413). T23n1435.

Sifen lü 四分律. Translated by Fotuoyeshe 佛陀耶舍 (Buddhayasás, fl. 401) and Zhu Fonian 竺佛念 (fl. 383). T22n1428.

Sifenlü shanfan buque xingshi chao 四分律刪繁補闕行事鈔. Composed by Daoxuan 道宣 (596–667). T40n1804.

Siku quanshu 四庫全書. 1773–1793. Edited by Ji Yun 紀昀 (1724–1805), et al. Beijing: Wenyuange. Rpt. ed. in 1,500 vols. Taibei: Shangwu yinshuguan, 1983–1986.

Shou xinsui jing 受新歲經. Translated by Dharmarakṣa (d. 308). T01n0061.

Taiping jing 太平經. Attributed to Yu Jie 于吉 (d. ca. AD 200). DZ 1101.

Taishang dongxuan lingbao benhang yinyuan jing 太上洞玄靈寶本行因緣經. Composed by Anonymous (fl. ca. 420). DZ1115.

Taishang dongxuan lingbao benhang suyuan jing 太上洞玄靈寶本行宿緣經. Composed by Anonymous during the Eastern Jin dynasty (316–420). DZ 1114.

Taishang dongxuan lingbao sanyuan yujing xuandu daxian jing 太上洞玄靈寶三元玉京玄都大獻經. Composed by Anonymous during the Northern and Southern Dynasties (420–589). DZ 370.

Taishang yisheng haikong zhizang jing 太上一乘海空智藏經. Composed by Anonymous (fl. ca. early to mid-seventh century). DZ 9.

Taizi ruiying benqi jing 太子瑞應本起經. Translated by Zhi Qian 支謙 (fl. ca. 223–252). T03n0185.

Xianyu jing 賢愚經. Translated by Huijue 慧覺 (fl. 445) et al. T04n0202.

Xiaojing zhushu 孝經注疏. Commentated by Xing Bing 邢昺 (932–1010). *Shisan jing zhushu* ed.

Xiuxing benqi jing 修行本起經. Translated by Zhu Dali 竺大力 (fl. AD 197) and Kang Mengxiang 康孟祥 (fl. AD 194). T03n0184.

Xu Gaoseng zhuan 續高僧傳. Compiled by Daoxuan 道宣 (596–667). T50n2060.

Yanshi jiaxun (zengbu ben) 顏氏家訓（增補本）. Written by Yan Zhitui 顏之推 (531–591), edited and annotated by Wang Liqi 王利器. Beijing: Zhonghua shuju, 1996.

Yiqie jing yinyi 一切經音義. Composed by Xuanying 玄應 (fl. 645). C056n1163.

Yiqie zhi guangming xianren cixin yinyuan bu shirou jing 一切智光明仙人慈心因緣不食肉經. Translated by Anonymous (fl. 350–431). T03n0183.

Yiwen leiju 藝文類聚. Compiled by Ouyang Xun 歐陽詢 (557--641). Modern Punctuated ed. in 2 vols, Shanghai: Shanghai guji chubanshe. 2007.

Yulanpen jing shu 盂蘭盆經疏. Composed by Zongmi 宗密 (780–841). T39n1792.

Yulanpen jing shu xiaoheng chao 盂蘭盆經疏孝衡鈔. Composed by Yurong 遇榮 (Song dynasty). X21n0375.

Za ahan jing 雜阿含經. Translated by Qiunabatuoluo 求那跋陀羅 (Guṇabhadra, 394–468). T02n0099.

Zengyi ahan jing 增壹阿含經. Translated by Sengqietipo 僧伽提婆 (Saṃghadeva, fl. 398). T02n0125.

Zhenzheng lun 甄正論. Composed by Xuanyi 玄嶷 (fl. 684–704). T52n2112.

Zhong ahan jing 中阿含經. Translated by Sengqietipo 僧伽提婆 (Saṃghadeva, fl. 398). T01n0026.

Zhongjing mulu 眾經目錄. Compiled by Fajing 法經 (fl. 594) et al. T55n2148.

Zhongjing mulu 眾經目錄. Compiled by Yancong 彥琮 (557–610) et al. T55n2147.

Zhouli zhushu 周禮注疏. Commentated by Zheng Xuan 鄭玄 (AD 127–200), sub-commentated by Jia Gongyan 賈公彥 (fl. mid-seventh century). *Shisan jing zhushu* edition.

Zhuanji baiyu jing 撰集百緣經. Translated by Zhi Qian 支謙 (fl. ca. 223–252). T04n0200.

Zhengtong daozang 正統道藏. Compiled by Zhang Yuchu 張宇初 (1361–1410) and Zhang Yuqing 張宇清 (d. 1426). Shanghai: Shangwu yinshuguan, 1923–1926. Rept. in 60 vols, Taibei: Yiwen yinshugua, 1977.

Zhenyuan xinding shijiao mulu 貞元新定釋教目錄. Compiled by Yuanzhao 圓照 (fl. 800). T55n2157.

Secondary Sources (list by author)

Adams, Douglas Q. 1988. *Tocharian Historical Phonology and Morphology*. New Haven, CT: American Oriental Society.

Akizuki, Kan'ei 秋月觀暎. 1961. 'Sangen shisō no keisei ni tsuite—Dōkyō no ōhō shisō' 道教の三元思想について——道教の応報思想. *Tōbo gaku* 東方學 22: 1–14.

———. 1965. '*Sairon sangen shisō no keisei: Sandō dōhō kakai eishi no seiritsu nendaiwo chūshin ni*' 再論三元思想の形成: 三洞奉道科戒営始の成立年代を中心に. *Hirosaki daigaku bunkyō rōnsō* 弘前大学文経論叢 1:437–456.

Allon, Mark. 1997a. 'The Oral Composition and Transmission of Early Buddhist Texts.' In *Indian Insights: Buddhism, Brahmanism and Bhakti. Papers from the Annual Spalding Symposium on Indian Religion*, edited by Peter Connolly and Sue Hamilton, 39–61. London: Luzac Oriental.

———. 1997b. *Style and Function: A Study of the Dominant Stylistic Features of the Prose Portions of Pali Canonical Sutta Texts and their Mnemonic Function*. Tokyo: International Institute for Buddhist Studies.

———. 2008. 'Recent Discoveries of Buddhist Manuscripts from Afghanistan and Pakistan and their Significance.' In *Art, Architecture and Religion: Along the Silk Roads*, edited by Kenneth Parry, 153–178. *Silk Road Studies 12*. Turnhout, Belgium: Brepols.

———. 2021. *The Composition and Transmission of Early Buddhist Texts with Specific Reference to Sutras*. Bochum/Freiburg: Projekt Verlag.

———. 2022. 'Early Buddhist Texts: Their Composition and Transmission.' *Journal of Indian philosophy* 2022: 1–34.

Bandō, Shōjun. 2005. 'Translator's Instruction.' In *Apocryphal Scriptures*, edited by Senkagu Mayeda, 17. Berkeley, CA: Numata Center for Buddhist Translation and Research.

Barrett, T. H. 2019. 'Translation and Transmission of Buddhist Texts.' London: British Library. 23 September 2019. https://www.bl.uk/sacred-texts/articles/translation-and-transmission-of-buddhism#authorBlock1.

BBASH (Berlin-Brandenburg Academy of Sciences and Humanities), ed. 2007. *Turfan Studies*. Berlin: Akademienvorhaben Turfanforschun. http://turfan.bbaw.de/bilder/Turfan_engl_07.pdf.

Beal, Samuel, trans. 1880. 'The Avalambana Sûtra.' *The Oriental*, 6 November 1875. Rept. in *Indian Antiquary, A Journal of Oriental Research in Archæology, History, Literature, Languages, Philosophy, Religion, Folklore, etc.* 9: 85–86.

———. 1904. *Si-Yu-Ki: Buddhist Records of the Western World, Translated from the Chinese of Hiuen Tsiang (A.D. 629) in Two Volumes*. London: Kegan Paul.

Bingenheimer, Marcus. 2011. *Studies in Āgama Literature – With Special Reference to the Shorter Chinese Saṃyuktāgama*. Taibei: Xinwenfen.

Bokenkamp, Stephen. 2008. 'Lingbao.' In *The Encyclopedia of Taoism, Volume 1: A–L*, edited by Fabrizio Pregadio, 663–667. London: Routledge.

Boucher, Daniel 2006. 'Dharmarakṣa and the Transmission of Buddhism to China.' *Asia Major* 19.1/2: 13–37.

———. 2016. 'Cāndhārī and the Early Chinese Buddhist Translations.' In *Cross-Cultural Transmission of Buddhist Texts: Theories and Practices of Translation*, edited by Dorji Wangchuk, 23–50. Hamburg: Department of Indian and Tibetan Studies, Universität Hamburg.

Bühler, George, trans. *2020. The Law of Manu*. Oxford: Clarendon Press, 1886. Digital ed. in Vol. XXV of *Sacred Books of the East*. Santa Cruz, CA: Evinity Publishing Inc. https://www.sacred-texts.com/hin/manu/manu09.htm.

Burlingame, Eugene Watson, trans. 2020. 'X. 7. Death of Moggallāna the Great/ Mahāmoggallānattheravatthu (137–140).' In 'Book X. The Rod or Punishment, Daṇḍa Vagga' of *Buddhist Legends: Translated from the Original Pāli Text of the Dhammapada Commentary*, translated by Eugene Watson Burlingame, proof-read by Ven. Khemaratana. Cambridge, MA: Harvard University Press, 1921. Digital ed., proof-read and prepared by Ānandajoti Bhikkhu. N.p.: Ancient Buddhist Texts. https://www.ancient-buddhist-texts.net/English-Texts/Buddhist-Legends/10-07.htm.

Buswell Jr., Robert E. 1990. 'Introduction.' In *Chinese Buddhist Apocrypha*, edited by Robert E. Buswell Jr., 1–30. Honolulu: University of Hawaii Press.

Buswell Jr., Robert E. and Donald S. Lopez Jr., eds. 2013. *The Princeton Dictionary of Buddhism*. Princeton, NJ: Princeton University Press.

Campany, Robert Ford. 2012. *Signs from the Unseen Realm: Buddhist Miracle Tales from Early Medieval China*. Honolulu: University of Hawai'i Press.

Chang, Kun. 1957. *A Comparative Study of the Kaṭhinavastu*. 's-Gravenhage: Mouton.

Chen, Fang-Ying 陳芳英. 1983. *Mulian jiumu gushi zhi yanjin jiqi youguan wenxue zhi yanjiu* 目連故事之演進及其有關文學之研究. Taibei: Guoli Taiwan daxue chuban weiyuanhui.

Chen, Hong 陳洪. 1999. 'Yulanpen hui qiyuan ji youguan wenti xintan' 盂蘭盆會起源及其有關問題新探. *Foxue yanjiu* 佛學研究 8: 239–246.

Ch'en, Kenneth K. S. 1964. *Buddhism in China: A Historical Survey*. Princeton: Princeton University Press.

———. 1968. 'Filial Piety in Chinese Buddhism.' *Harvard Journal of Asiatic Studies* 28: 81–97.

———. 1973. *The Chinese Transformation of Buddhism*. Princeton, NJ: Princeton University Press.

Chen, Tsu-Lung 陳祚龍. 1987. 'Kanle Dunhuang guchao *Foshuo Yulanpeng jing* yihou' 看了敦煌古抄「佛說盂蘭盆經讃述」以後. *Dunhuang xue* 敦煌學 12: 13–82.

Cole, Alan. 1998. *Mothers and Sons in Chinese Buddhism*. Stanford, CA: Stanford University Press.

Deeg, Max. 2008. 'Creating Religious Terminology – A Comparative Approach to Early Chinese Buddhist Translations.' *Journal of the International Association of Buddhist Studies* 31.1/2: 83–118.

Delhey, Martin. 2016. 'From Sanskrit to Chinese and Back Again: Remarks on Xuanzang's Translations of the Yogācārabhūmi and Closely Related Philosophical Treatises.' In *Cross-Cultural Transmission of Buddhist Texts: Theories and Practices of Translation*, edited by Dorji Wangchuk, 51–79. Hamburg: Department of Indian and Tibetan Studies, Universität Hamburg.

Demoto, Mitsuyo 出本充代. 1998. '*Avadānaśataka* no Bon Kan hikaku kenkyū' *Avadānaśataka* の梵漢比較研究. PhD thesis, Kyoto University, Japan.

Dhammananda, K. Sri, ed. 1996. *Faju jing gushi ji* 法句經故事集, translated by Zhou Jinyan 周金言. Jiayi, Taiwan: Xinyu zazhishe.

Dunn, James Douglas Grant. 2013. *The Oral Gospel Tradition*. Cambridge, England: W. B. Eerdmans Publishers.

Eitel, Ernest John. 1904. *Handbook for the Student of Chinese Buddhism*. London: Trubner & Co., 1870. Rev. and enl. ed. Tokyo: Sanshushan.

Fâ-Hien (aka. Faxian 法顯, ca. 337–422). 2019. *A Record of Buddhistic Kingdoms: Being an Account by the Chinese Monk Fâ-Hien of His Travels in India and Ceylon (A.D. 399–414) in Search of the Buddhist Books of Discipline*, translated and annotated by James Legge (1815–1897). Oxford: Clarendon Press, 1886. Digital ed. Lismore: The Buddha Dharma Education Association Inc. http://www.buddhanet.net/pdf_file/rbddh10.pdf.

Feng, Jiasheng 冯家昇. 1962. 'Yijiuwujiu nian Hami xin faxian de Huihuwen Fojing' 1959 年哈密新发現的回鶻文佛經. *Wenwu* 文物 7–8: 90–97.

Fouw, Hart de. and Robert E. Svoboda. 2003. *Light on Life: An Introduction to the Astrology of India*. Rept. ed. Twin Lakes, WI: Lotus Press.

Fujimoto, Akira 藤本晃. 2003. '*BussetsuUrabon-kyō* no genryū—Petavatthu 2.2 "Sharihotsu Haha gakiji" to no hikaku kōstsu' 『仏説盂蘭盆経』の源流——Petavatthu 2.2「舎利弗母餓鬼事」との比較考察. *Pārigaku Bukkyō bunkagaku* パーリ学仏教文化学 17: 47–54.

Fujino, Ryunen 藤野立然. 1956. '*Urabon-kyō* kō' 《盂蘭盆経》攷. *Ryūkoku daigaku ronshū* 龍谷大學論集 353: 340–345.

Ganguli, Kisari Mohan. 1883–1896. *Mahabharata of Krishna-Dwaipayana Vyasa: Translated into English Prose from the Original Sanskrit Text, Book 1: Adi Parva*. Calcutta: Bharata Press.

Gehman, Henry Snyder, trans. 1974. 'Petavatthu: Stories of the Departed.' In *The Mino Anthologies of the Pali Canon*, Part IV, edited by Rhys Davids. London: Luzac & Co., 1942. Rept. ed. London: Pāli Text Society.

Harrison, Paul. 1998. 'Women in the Pure Land: Some Reflections on the Textual Sources.' *Journal of Indian Philosophy* 26.6: 553–572.

Hendrischke, Barbara. 2006. *The Scripture on Great Peace: The Taiping jing and the Beginnings of Daoism*. Berkeley and Los Angeles: University of California Press.

Hinsch, Bret. 2002. 'Confucian Filial Piety and the Construction of the Ideal Chinese Buddhist Woman.' *Journal of Chinese Religions* 30.1: 49–75.

Hiroshi, Maruyama. 2008. '*daochang*' 道場. In *The Encyclopedia of Taoism, Volume 1: A–L*, edited by Fabrizio Pregadio, 310–311. London: Routledge.

Holt, John. 2017. *Theravada Traditions: Buddhist Ritual Cultures in Contemporary Southeast Asia and Sri Lanka*. Honolulu: University of Hawaii Press.

Honda, Giei 本田義英. 1927. 'Urabon kyō to Jōdo urabon kyō' 盂蘭盆經と浄土盂蘭盆經. *Ryūkoku daigaku ronsō* 龍谷大学論叢 276: 1–21. Kyoto: Ryūkoku daigaku ronsōsha.

Hsiao, Teng-fu 蕭登福. 1995. *Daojiao yu Fojiao* 道教與佛教. Taibei: Dongda tushu gongsi.

———. 1996. 'Lun Fojiao shou Zhongtu Daojiao de yingxiang ji Fojing zhenwei' 論佛教受中土道教的影響及佛經真偽. *Zhonghua foxue xuebao* 中華佛學學報 9: 83–98.

———. 2005. *Daojiao Daojia yingxiang xia de Fojiao jingdian* 道教道家影響下的佛教經典. Taibei: Xinwenfeng chuban gongsi.

Hu, Shi 胡適. 1986. 'Shuo ru' 說儒. In Vol. 15 of *Hu Shi zuoping ji* 胡適作品集, edited by Zhan Hongzhi 詹宏志, 99–159. Taibei: Yuanliu chuban.

Hua, Hsüan. 1998. *Dharma Talks in Europe: Given by the Venerable Master Hua in 1990.* Ukiah, CA: Buddhist Text Translation Society.

Hureau, Sylvie. 2009. 'Translations, Apocrypha, and the Emergence of the Buddhist Canon.' In *Early Chinese Religion, Part Two: The Period of Division*, edited by John Lagerwey and Pengzhi Lü, 763–773. Leiden: Brill.

I-Tsing (aka Yijing 義淨, 635–713). 1896. *A Record of the Buddhist Religion: As Practised in India and the Malay Archipelago (A.D. 671–695)*, translated by J. Takakusu. Oxford: Clarendon Press.

Ikeda, Chotatsu 池田澄達. 1926. '*Urabon-kyō* ni tsuite' 《盂蘭盆経》に就いて. *Shūkyō kenkyū* 宗教研究 3.1: 59–64.

Imoto, Eiichi 井本英一. 1966. 'Urabon no sho mondai' 盂蘭盆の諸問題. *Oriento* オリエント 9.1: 41–66, 92.

Irisawa, Takashi 入澤崇. 1990. 'Bussetsu urabon kyō seiritsu kō' 仏説盂蘭盆経成立考. *Bukkyōgaku kenkyū* 仏教學研究 45–46: 145–172.

Iwamoto, Yutaka 岩本裕. 1968. *Mokuren densetsu to urabon* 目連伝説と盂蘭盆. Kyoto: Hōzōkan.

———. 1979. *Bukkyō setsuwa kenkyū* 仏教説話研究. In Vol. 4 of *Jigoku menuri no bungaku* 地獄めぐりの文学. Tokyo: Kaimei shoten.

Jia, Jinhua. 2022. 'Translation and Interaction: A New Examination of the Controversy over the Translation and Authenticity of the *Śūraṃgama-sūtra*.' *Religions* 13.6: 474. https://doi.org/10.3390/rel13060474.

Ji, Xianlin. 2011. *Fragments of the Tocharian A Maitreyasamiti-Nāṭaka of the Xinjiang Museum, China.* Berlin: De Gruyter Mouton.

Johnson, David, ed. 1989. *Ritual Opera, Operatic Ritual: 'Mu-lien Rescues His Mother in Chinese Popular Culture.* Berkeley, CA: The Chinese Popular Culture Project.

Julien, Stanislas. 1861. *Méthode pour déchiffrer et transcrire les noms sanscrits qui se rencontrent dans les livres chinois, à l'aide des règles, d'exercices et d'un répertoire de onze cents caractères chinois idéographiques, employés alphabétiquement.* Paris: Imprimerie impériale.

Kapstein, Matthew T. 2007. 'Mulian in the Land of Snows and King Gesar in Hell: A Chinese Tale of Parental Death in Its Tibetan Transformations.' In *The Buddhist Dead: Practice, Discourse, Representations*, edited by Bryan J. Cuevas and Jacqueline Ilyes Stone, 345–377. Honolulu: University of Hawai'i Press.

Karashima, Seishi. 2013a. 'A Study of the Language of Early Chinese Buddhist Translations: A Comparison between the Translations by Lokakṣema and Zhi Qian.' *Annual Report of The International Research Institute for Advanced Buddhology at Soka University (ARIRLAB)* 16: 273–288.

———. 2013b. 'The Meaning of *Yulanpen* 盂蘭盆—"Rice Bowl" on *Pravāraṇa* Day.' *ARIRIAB* 16: 289–305.

Kohn, Livia. 2009. *Readings in Daoist Mysticism*. Magdalena, NM: Three Pine Press.

Kornicki, Peter Francis. 2018. 'The Chinese Buddhist Canon and Other Buddhist Texts.' In *Languages, scripts, and Chinese texts in East Asia*, edited by Kornicki, Peter Francis, 217–245. Oxford: Oxford University Press.

Kumar, Yukteshwar. 2005. *A History of Sino-Indian Relations: 1st Century A.D. to 7th Century A.D.: Movement of Peoples and Ideas Between India and China from Kasyapa Matanga to Yi Jing*. New Dehli: APH Publishing Corporation.

Langer, Rita. 2007. *Buddhist Rituals of Death and Rebirth: Contemporary Sri Lankan Practice and Its Origins*. Abingdon, England: Routledge.

Lardinois, Roland. 1996. 'The World Order and the Family Institution in India.' In Vol. 1 of *A History of the Family*, edited by André Burguière et al., 566–600. Cambridge, MA: Belknap Press.

Leumann, Ernst. 1919. *Maitreya-samiti, das Zukunftsideal der Buddhisten*. Strassburg: Karl J. Trübner.

Liang, Qichao 梁啟超 (1920–1924). 1999. *Fanyi wenxue yu Fodian* 翻譯文學與佛典. In Vol. 13 of *Liang Qichao quanji* 梁啟超全集, edited by Liang, Qichao 梁啟超, 3715–4002. Beijing: Beijing chubanshe.

Liao, Ben 廖奔. 1995. 'Mulian shimo' 目連始末. *Minsu quyi* 民俗曲藝 93: 1–30.

Liu, Zhen 劉 震 and Wang Rujuan 王 汝 娟. 2016. 'Hewei "Daochang (Bodhimaṇḍa)?" ' 何謂「道場」(Bodhimaṇḍa)? *Foguang xuebao* 佛光學報 2: 189–228.

Lopez Jr., Donald S. 2016. *The Lotus Sūtra: A Biography*. Princeton and London: Princeton University Press.

Lü, Pengzhi. 2011. 'The Lingbao Fast of the Three Primes and the Daoist Middle Prime Festival: A Critical Study of the "Taishang Dongxuan Lingbao Sanyuan Pinjie Jing".' *Cahiers d'Extrême-Asie* 20: 35–61.

Lüders, Heinrich. 1911. 'Das Sāriputraprakaraṇa, ein Drama des Aśvaghoṣa.' *Sitzungsberichte der Königlich Preussischen Akademie der Wissenschaften zu Berlin* 17: 388–411.

Lung, Rachel. 2016. 'A Cultural Approach to the Study of Xuanzang.' In *Cross-Cultural Transmission of Buddhist Texts: Theories and Practices of Translation*, edited by Dorji Wangchuk, 99–117. Hamburg: Department of Indian and Tibetan Studies, Universität Hamburg.

Ma, Zuyi 馬祖毅. 1984. *Zhongguo fanyi jianshi* 中國翻譯簡史. Beijing: Zhongguo fanyi chuban gongsi.

Mair, Victor H. 1986–1987. 'Notes on the Maudgalyāyana Legend in East Asia.' *Monumental Serica* 37: 83–89.

———. 1989. *T'ang Transformation Texts: A Study of the Buddhist Contribution to the Rise of Vernacular Fiction and Drama in China*. Cambridge, MA: Harvard University Press.

Mak, Bill M. 2016. 'Matching Stellar Ideas to the Stars: Remarks on the Translation of Indian *jyotiṣa* in the Chinese Buddhist Canon.' In *Cross-Cultural Transmission of Buddhist Texts: Theories and Practices of Translation*, edited by Dorji Wangchuk, 139–158. Hamburg: Department of Indian and Tibetan Studies, Universität Hamburg.

Makita, Tairyō 牧田諦亮. 1976. *Gikyō kenkyū* 疑経研究. Kyoto: Kyoto daigaku jinbun kagaku kenkyūju.

———. 1985. 'Yijing yanjiu – Zhongguo Fojiao zhong zhi zhenjing yu yijing' 疑經研究——中國佛教中之真經與疑經, translated by Yang Baiyi 楊白衣. *Hua-Kang Buddhist Journal* 4: 284–304.

Mei, Naiwen 梅迺文. 1996. 'Zhu Fahu de fanyi chutan' 竺法護的翻譯初探. *Zhonghua foxue xuebao* 中華佛學學報 9: 49–64.

Michihata, Ryoshii 道端良秀. 1973. *Fojiao yu Rujia lunli* 佛教與儒家倫理, translated by Monk Huiyue 慧嶽. Taibei: Zhonghua Fojiao wenxian bianzuanshe.

———. 1986. *Chūigoku bukyō to jukyō rinri kō to no kyōshō* 中国仏教と儒教倫理孝との交渉. Tokyo: Shoen.

Miyakawa, Hasayuki 宮川尚志. 1964. *Rikuchōshi kenkyū* 六朝史研究. Kyoto: Heirakuji shoten.

Mizuno, Kogen 水野弘元. 1970. 'Betsuyaku agon kyō ni tsuite' 別訳雑阿含経について. *Indogaku Bukkyōgaku kenkyū* 印度学仏教学研究 18.2: 41–51.

Monier-Williams, M. 2003. *A Sanskrit-English Dictionary: Etymologically and Philologically Arranged with Special Reference to Cognate Indo-European Languages.* Oxford: Clarendon Press, 1989. Digital ed. Cologne: Cologne Digital Sanskrit Lexicon. http://faculty.washington.edu/prem/mw/mw.html.

Muller, Charles. 1998. 'East Asian Apocryphal Scriptures: Their Origin and Role in the Development of Sinitic Buddhism.' *Bulletin of Toyo Gakuen University* 6: 63–73.

Nanjio, Bunyiu. 1883. *A Catalogue of the Chinese Translation of Buddhist Tripitaka, the Sacred Canon of the Buddhist in China and Japan.* Oxford: Clarendon Press.

Nattier, Jan. 2008. *A Guide to the Earliest Chinese Buddhist Translations: Texts from the Eastern Han and Three Kingdoms Periods.* Tokyo: The International Research Institute for Advanced Buddhology (IRIAB), Soka University.

———. 2014. 'Now You Hear it, Now You Don't: The Phrase "Thus Have I Heard" in Early Chinese Buddhist Translations.' In Vol. 1 of *Buddhism across Asia: Networksof Material, Intellectual and Cultural Exchange*, edited by Tansen Sen, 39–64, Singapore: The Institute of Southeast Asian Studies (ISEAS).

Nida, Eugene A. and Charles R. Taber. 1969. *The Theory and Practice of Translation, with Special Reference to Bible Translation.* Leiden: Brill.

Ōfuchi, Ninji 大淵忍爾. 1985. 'Dōkyō ni okeru sangen setsu no seiei to tenkai' 道教における三元説の生成と展開. *Tōhō shūkyō* 東方宗教 66: 1–21.

Ogawa, Kan'ichi 小川 貫弌. 1964. 'Mukuren kyūbo henbun no genryū' 目連救母変文の源流. *Bukkyō bungaku kenkyū* 仏教文学研究 2: 7–46.

———. 1973. *Bukkyō bunka shi kenkyū* 仏教文化史研究. Kyoto: Nagata bunshōdō.

Palumbo, Antonello. 1997. 'On the Author and Date of *Zhenzheng Lun* 甄正論: An obscure Page in the Struggle between Buddhists and Taoists in Medieval China.' *Annali dell'Università degli Studi di Napoli "L'Orientale"* 57.3/4: 305–322.

———. 2013. *An Early Chinese Commentary on the* Ekottarika-āgama: *The* Fenbie gongde lun 分別功德論 *and the History of the Translation of the* Zengyi ahan jing 增一阿含經. Taibei: Dharma Drum Publishing Corporation.

Penner, Hans H. 2009. 'Devadatta Attempts to Kill the Buddha'. In *Rediscovering the Buddha: Legends of the Buddha and Their Interpretation*, edited by Penner, Hans H., 85–90. New York: Oxford University Press.

Qing, Xitai 卿希泰, ed. 1990. *Daojiao yu Zhongguo chuantong wenhua* 道教與中國傳統文化. Fuzhou: Fujian renmin chubanshe.

Sayers, Matthew R. 2013. *Feeding the Dead: Ancestor Worship in Ancient India.* New York: Oxford University Press.

Schipper, Kristofer (aka Shi Bo'er 施博爾; Shi Zhouren 施舟人). 1977. *Zhengtong Daozang mulu suoyin* 正統道藏目錄索引. Taibei: Yiwen yinshuguan.

Schopen, Gregory. 1984. 'Filial Piety and the Monk in the Practice of Indian Buddhism: A Question of "Sinicization" Viewed from the Other Side.' *T'oung Pao* 70.1–3: 110–126.

Sieg, Emil and Wilhelm Siegling. 1921. *Tocharische Sprachreste*. Berlin-Leipzig: Walter de Gruyter.

Storch, Tanya. 2015. 'Fei Changfang's *Records of the Three Treasures Throughout the Successive Dynasties* (*Lidai sanbao ji*) and Its Role in the Formation of the Chinese Buddhist Canon.' In *Spreading Buddha's Word in East Asia: The Formation and Transformation of the Chinese Buddhist Canon*, edited by Jiang Wu and Lucille Chia, 109–142. New York: Columbia University Press.

Strong, John. 1983. 'Filial Piety and Buddhism: The Indian Antecedents to a "Chinese" Problem.' In *Traditions in Contact and Change*, edited by Peter Slater and Donald Wiebe, 171–186. Waterloo: Wilfred Laurier University Press.

Tan, Piya, trans. 2011. 'The *Māra TajjanīyaSutta/The Discourse on the Rebuking of Māra* (M 50): Moggallāna's Past Life as Māra Dūsī.' In Vol. 36.4 of the Sutta Discovery Series, 114–126. PDF version, Singapore: The Minding Centre. http://www.themindingcentre.org/dharmafarer/wp-content/uploads/2010/02/36.4-Mara-Tajjaniya-S-m50-piya.pdf

Tang, Yongtong 湯用彤. 1983. 'Du *Taipingjing* suojian' 讀《太平經》所見. In *Tang Yongtong xueshu lunwen ji* 湯用彤學術論文集, edited by Tang, Yongtong 湯用彤, 52–79. Beijing: Zhonghua shuju.

———. 2006. '*Taiping jing* yu Fojiao' 《太平經》與佛教. In *Han Wei Liangjin Nanbeichao Fojiao shi* 漢魏兩晉南北朝佛教史, edited by Tang, Yongtong 湯用彤, 95–108. Enl. ed. in 2 vols. Beijing: Kunlun chubanshe.

Teiser, Stephen F. 1986. 'Ghosts and Ancestors in Medieval Chinse Religion: The Yü-lan-p'en Festival as Mortuary Ritual.' *History of Religion* 26.1: 47–67.

———. 1988. *The Ghost Festival in Medieval China*. Princeton, NJ: Princeton University Press.

———. 1989. 'The Ritual behind the Opera: A Fragmentary Ethnography of the Ghost Festival, A.D. 400–1900'. In *Ritual Opera, Operatic Ritual: 'Mu-lien Rescues His Mother in Chinese Popular Culture*, edited by David Johnson, 191–223. Berkeley, CA: The Chinese Popular Culture Project.

Tillakaratne, M.P. 1986. *Manners, Customs and Ceremonies of Sri Lanka*. Delhi: Sri Satguru Publications.

Tokuno, Kyoko. 1990. 'The Evaluation of Indigenous Scriptures in Chinese Buddhist Bibliographical Catalogues.' In *Chinese Buddhist Apocrypha*, edited by Robert E. Buswell Jr., 31–74. Honolulu: University of Hawaii Press.

Tsuchiya, Taisuke 土屋太祐. 2005. '*Yulanpen wenxian suo fanying de Zhongtu minjian Xinyang ruogan gainian de xin bianhua* 盂蘭盆文獻所反映的中土民間信仰若干概念的新變化. *Xinguoxue* 新國學 00.189–212.

Walters, Jonathan S. 1990. 'The Buddha's Bad Karma: A Problem in the History of Theravâda Buddhism.' *Numen* 37.1: 70–95.

Wang, Chongming 王翀名. 2017. 'Da Mujianlian xingxiang zhi yanjiu – yi Hanyi Fodian wei hexin' 大目犍連形象之研究——以漢譯佛典為核心. MA thesis, Soochow University, Taibei.

Wang, Wenyan 王文顏. 1997. *Fodian yiweijing yanjiu yu kaolu* 佛典疑偽經研究與考錄. Taibei: Wenjin.

Wu, Zhen 吳震. 1960. 'Hami faxian dapi Huihuwen xiejing' 哈密發現大批回鶻文寫經. *Wenwu* 文物 5: 85–86.

Wu, Mingyuan 吳明遠. 2001. 'Zhongguo wu liu shiji Yulanpenhui zhi tanyuan' 中國五、六世紀盂蘭盆會之探源. MA thesis, National Taiwan University, Taibei.

Xing, Guang. 2011. 'Yulanpen Festival and Chinese Ancestor Worship.' *JCBSSL: Journal of the Centre for Buddhist Studies, Sri Lanka* (*Journal of Buddhist Studies*) 9: 123–142.

———. 2012. 'Buddhist Influence on Chinese Religions and Popular Beliefs.' *International Journal of Buddhist Thought & Culture* 18: 135–157.

———. 2016. 'The Teaching and Practice of Filial Piety in Buddhism.' *Journal of Law and Religion* 31.2: 212–226.

Xiong, Juan 熊娟. 2014. '"*Yulanpen*" de yuyuan yuyi kaocha'「盂蘭盆」的語源語義考察. *Hanyu shi xuebao* 漢語史學報 14: 85–104.

———. 2015. '*Yulanpen jing* de yuliao jianbie' 《盂蘭盆經》語料鑒別. In *Hanwen fodian yiweijing yanjiu* 漢文佛典疑偽經研究, edited by Xiong, Juan 熊娟, 247–289. Shanghai: Shanghai guji chubanshe.

Xu, Dishan 許地山. 1927. 'Fanju tili jiqi zai Hanju shang di diandian didi' 梵劇體例及其在漢劇上底點點滴滴. *Xiaoshuo yuebao* 小說月報 17 (Special Issue): 1–36.

Yin, Guangming 殷光明. 2006. *Dunhuang bihua yishu yu yiwei jing* 敦煌壁畫藝術與疑偽經. Beijing: Minzu chubanshe.

Yoshikawa, Yoshikazu 吉川良和. 2003. '*Kyūbo kyō* to *Kyūbo hōkan* no Mokuren mono ni kansuru setsuchō geinō teki shiron 『救母経』と『救母宝巻』の目連物に関する説唱芸能的試論. *Hitotsubashi daigakukenkyū nenpō· Shakaigaku kenkyū* 一橋大学研究年報·社会学研究 41: 61–135.

Yoshioka, Yoshitoyo 吉岡義豐. 1970. 'Chūgen urabon no dōkyō teki kōsatsu 中元盂蘭盆の道教的考察'. In *Dōkyō to bukkyō daini* 道教と仏教（第2), edited by Yoshioka Yoshitoyo 吉岡義豐 231–286. Tokyo: Toshima shobō.

Yüsüp, Israpil, et al., eds. 1988. *Qädimki Uyġur yeziġidiki Maitrisimit/ Maitrisimit nom bitig* (*Huihu wen* Mile huijian ji). Urumqi: Šinǧan Ḫalq Nešriyati/Xinjiang remin chubanshe.

Zhan, Ru. 2019. 'Mahāsāṃghika and Mahāyāna: An Analysis of Faxian and the Translation of the *Mahāsāṃghika Vinaya* (Chin. *Mohe Sengqi Lü*).' *Hualin International Journal of Buddhist Studies* 2.1: 302–324.

Zhang, Miao 張淼. 2006. 'Fojing yiweijing sixiang yanjiu – yi Fojing jinglu wei zhongxin de kaocha' 佛經疑偽經思想研究——以佛經經錄為中心的考察. PhD thesis, Nanjing, China.

Zhang, Xun 章巽. 1985. *Faxian zhuan jiaozhu* 法顯傳校注. Shanghai: Shanghai guji chubanshe.

Zhao, Xiaohuan. 2021a. *Chinese Theatre: An Illustrated History Through Nuoxi and Mulianxi – Volume One: From Exorcism to Entertainment.* London and New York: Routledge.

———. 2021b. *Chinese Theatre: An Illustrated History Through Nuoxi and Mulianxi – Volume Two: From Storytelling to Story-acting.* London and New York: Routledge.

Zhu, Hengfu 朱恆夫. 1987. '*Foshuo Yulanpen jing* de yingxiang yu dui gaijing zhenwei de kangfa'《佛說盂蘭盆經》的影響與對該經真偽的看法. *Shijie zongjiao yanjiu* 世界宗教研究 28.2: 54–59.

———. 1993. *Mulianxi yanjiu* 目連戲研究. Nanjing: Nanjing daxue chubanshe.

Zürcher, Erik. 1980. 'Buddhist Influence on Early Taoism: A Survey of Scriptural Evidence.' *T'oung Pao* 66.1–3: 84–147.

———. 1996. 'Vernacular Elements in Early Buddhist Texts: An Attempt to Define the Optimal Source Materials.' In Erik Zürcher, et al. 'Vernacularisms in Medieval Chinese.' *Sino-Platonic Papers* 71: 1–31.

INDEX

Printed in the USA
CPSIA information can be obtained
at www.ICGtesting.com
JSHW021315250823
47058JS00001B/1

9 781839 986963